NOTHING TO LOSE

UNLIKELY ALLIES IN THE STRUGGLE FOR A BETTER BLACK AMERICA

PASTOR DARRELL SCOTT

Post Hill
PRESS

A POST HILL PRESS BOOK
ISBN: 978-1-64293-465-6
ISBN (eBook): 978-1-64293-466-3

Post Hill Press
New York • Nashville
posthillpress.com
Published in the United States of America

CONTENTS

ONE

"**W**hat makes you think black people will vote for you? Word on the street is, you're a racist."

Those were my first words to Donald J. Trump. His answer would alter my view of him and put me on a journey that I never expected.

It was 2011, and Trump was considering a run against President Barack Obama in the 2012 presidential election. The real estate mogul wanted to gauge his support among evangelicals, both white and black. So he gathered some into a crowded conference room on the twenty-fifth floor of Trump Tower. As far as I can tell, no one has ever discussed this meeting in print before.

Here's how it all went down: Pastor Paula White, a longtime spiritual advisor and friend of Donald Trump, phoned me. Paula has many friends in the black churches, including me. I knew that she was conducting lunchtime Bible studies in Trump Tower. What I didn't know at the time is that sometimes Trump would drop by. He had become more curious spiritually as he had grown older. It was a personal transformation, the beginning of a spiritual journey, and the media was unaware of it.

At that time, Paula owned a unit in Trump Tower. How she came to own it is a story that reveals a hidden side of Trump. She told me that years earlier, Trump had told her that he had a unit available in the Tower and asked if she was interested. She told him that she was interested, but the price was way out of her reach. Preachers don't usually make enough money to afford a condo in Trump Tower.

Hearing her reply, Trump said, "I'll see what I can do to help you." He contacted the company sponsoring his speaking tour and suggested that it offer Paula a contract as a part of his tour. She earned a nice sum for each speaking engagement. Sometimes she spoke several times per month. She set the money aside, and after about a year she had earned enough money to purchase the unit. Trump didn't give her the money or cut the price, nor did she ask him to. She did not want to infringe upon their friendship, nor try to capitalize on her spiritual influence over him. He created an opportunity for her to earn that money, and she worked very hard in doing so.

When Paula phoned me, she said: "I wonder if you and Belinda can meet me in New York? I have some things I want to talk to you about." Belinda is my wife, and it was no problem for us to go. Paula had been our friend for many years and had spoken at my church many times. I didn't know what the conversation in New York would be about, but our friendship was such that I didn't feel the need to know in advance. Belinda and I would simply wait until we got there to find out.

So Belinda and I flew to New York. After we met Paula downstairs in the lobby of Trump Tower, she escorted us to a large conference room on the twenty-fifth floor—the very room seen on *The Celebrity Apprentice*. A long table dominated the room, and the windows offered a commanding view of New York's forest of skyscrapers.

The others in the room were just as impressive as the view; it was a veritable Who's Who of black and white church leaders. Televangelists. Christian book publishers. Gospel singers. Television network owners and program hosts. Some very large personalities in the Christian world. I won't name them here, because to this day a lot of them haven't divulged their attendance.

While we were all exchanging pleasantries, Donald Trump walked in. I wasn't expecting that. I don't think anyone else in the room was either.

At first I thought he was just going to say hello to Paula and the rest of us, and then leave. Instead, he started talking to all of us. He said, "I asked Paula to ask some of her friends to come here because I'm thinking about running for president in 2012."

I was shocked. This guy was thinking about running for president?

Trump continued, "I asked Paula to invite some of her friends here that she believes are in contact with God, so that you guys can pray for me that God gives me the wisdom to make the right decision as to whether I run or not."

I never thought of Trump as humble enough to ask for prayers. His television personality displays self-confidence and even brashness, but in that moment, he was asking Christians for prayer.

This was unexpected. I wasn't an avid watcher of *The Apprentice*, because I primarily watched Christian television, and I wasn't a hard-core Trump fan. But I was familiar with who Trump was. In fact, I liked his brand, which I knew was synonymous with luxury. I had stayed at the Trump hotel in Florida. I even owned a vintage Trump watch, which I still have. I once had a Trump mattress that I slept on very well.

Trump stood and bowed his head. We all prayed over him. It was a solemn moment. Together we prayed: "Lord, give him the wisdom to make the right decision. Lead him in the right direction. Let Your will be done regarding this matter."

No one pulled out a phone to record it for social media. In that moment, Trump was just an ordinary guy who was requesting prayer, like any person who comes to church and desires prayer. That impressed me.

Afterward, he sat down to talk. We sat there for five hours, talking about our Christian culture, our country, national and international issues both big and small. No topic was off-limits.

Trump opined that conditions in our country could be much better. He talked about U.S. Supreme Court seats and the need for federal judges who were conservative and respected the Constitution. I was impressed by the breadth of his knowledge, which ranged from economics and defense to social issues and poverty. Then one preacher said something I would never forget—something that would come true later:

"I want you to know one thing. If you decide to run for president, you're going to be the target of a Satanic attack like you've never seen before."

Trump was unlearned in our Christian vernacular, our Christian mode of conversation. He was kind of taken aback. "I mean, you're telling me the devil is going to attack me if I run?" He didn't quite know what to make of it. I don't know whether he believed it or not. He found the comment interesting, however. He nodded and continued talking.

Then, Trump acknowledged me.

Now, anyone who knows me knows I'm outspoken. I can be blunt. I can be candid—sometimes to my own detriment. It's hard for me to suppress my thoughts and feelings in an open dialogue. I'm not a loose cannon, though.

I looked right into his eyes and said, "Let me ask you a question. What makes you think black people will vote for you for president? Word on the street is, you're a racist."

Trump looked right back at me and didn't blink, flinch, or hesitate. "I'm the least racist person you ever want to meet," he said. "In my line of work, in what I do, I can't be a racist. I work with all kinds of people in all walks of life."

I waited for the rest of the explanation, for the standard "I had a black friend when I was in the third grade" or "We had a black maid" or "I know a lot of black people. I like black people; some of my best friends are black."

He never said any of that. He didn't pander, didn't bend over backward trying to convince me he wasn't racist. He just continued being himself. It caught me off guard, because I had been expecting him to try to persuade me that he was not a racist.

Trump considered it self-evident that he was not a racist, that the allegation just wasn't serious. He wasn't going to waste any time trying to explain why he didn't have two heads or why he wasn't a racist. He dismissed the idea entirely.

Something about his words and manner—the sense and spirit of it—made me realize that I liked the guy. He was open and honest.

He sat and talked with us for hours. He was in no hurry to leave. He knew a lot more than I gave him credit for, too. And he knew himself. He was not just a stereotypical elitist billionaire.

Barack Obama, president at the time, hadn't changed the lives of the black community. Black utopia hadn't come. Now I was being offered another choice. I liked Trump—I liked his personality, directness, and honesty. I also liked his opinions regarding the state of the country.

As for qualifications, I wasn't concerned. Obama had become president with little experience. He had been a first-term senator who hadn't even finished his term. Before that, he was a part-time lawmaker in Springfield, Illinois, and a part-time lecturer at the University of Chicago. All things considered, Trump was just as qualified as the last guy.

I walked out of that Trump Tower conference room with a different perspective, not only about Donald Trump but about the leadership and direction of our country as well.

Near the lobby elevator, one of the departing preachers said to me: "I like your boldness. You said that to Donald Trump's face about him being a racist?"

I replied, "I didn't come up here to kiss up to Donald Trump. Donald Trump didn't ask me up here to kiss up to him. Believe me, if Donald Trump wants to be kissed up to, he doesn't need me or anybody from Cleveland coming up here to do it."

I put my cards on the table. I didn't have any reason not to.

Michael Cohen, one of Trump's lawyers, came over and introduced himself to me, saying, "You know the boss, he likes that. He likes the fact that you were blunt and outspoken with him like that. He liked that about you."

Trump came over to say goodbye. "Hey, you're asking tough questions, huh?"

"Hey, you're a tough guy." I was only telling the truth.

"Let's stay in touch. Get his number, Michael."

Cohen and I agreed to stay in touch, beginning a friendship with many ups and downs.

He called me a few weeks later. "The boss decided not to run."

"Man, that's too bad," I responded. "I'm disappointed, because I would have liked for him to have run. I like the guy. I think he would have done a good job, based on our conversations. But let's stay in touch."

Over the years, Cohen and I stayed in contact. He called me brother minister, and I called him counselor. I liked him very much, and I think the feeling was mutual. I would always ask, "How's the big guy doing?"

He was always upbeat when it came to Trump. "He's doing great," he would say. "Stop up and see us sometime whenever you're in New York."

* * *

Fast-forward to 2015. I got a call from Cohen: "The boss is thinking about running. Turn your TV on."

I turned on my TV just as Trump was coming down the escalator. Cohen didn't waste a second: "You in?"

"Heck yeah, I'm in!"

"Let's put together another meeting with pastors like the one we had a few years ago. I'll call Paula up," Cohen said. "You bring some guys on your end—whoever you want to bring."

This time, however, the meeting was different.

We went back to Trump Tower, and there were a lot more people in the room this time—a lot of preachers who prefer to remain anonymous, even to this day.

I took some guys with me, including Pastor Mark Burns from South Carolina. He didn't know much about Donald Trump. He later became a CNN regular as a Trump "surrogate."

We arrived at Trump Tower to find a mixture of black and white preachers and Christian personalities. The conversation was largely the same as during the previous meeting: the U.S. Supreme Court, gun control, abortion, and so on.

When it came to the black preachers in the room, however, we were determined to ask hard questions. "What do you think of Black Lives Matter?"

Trump didn't miss a beat. "Listen, black lives do matter. White lives matter too. The Black Lives Matter organization has some good points, and they have some bad points."

He didn't elaborate.

We kept firing questions at him. "What do you think about the fact that the police are out here killing black people?"

Trump was direct. "Listen. I wonder sometimes if the police feel that the use of deadly force is necessary. Why do they shoot to kill? Why don't they shoot to disable? Why don't they shoot an arm or a leg?"

Okay, that was pretty interesting. It was a unique perspective. It again showed that he was not pandering. I could tell that he was giving thought to each question, and that his observations were coming from a place of personal honesty.

We kept hitting him with questions. "Well, what about the inner cities?"

"I believe that the sources of a number of the problems that the black community faces are unemployment, underemployment, lack of quality education, and depressed living conditions.... If we could provide jobs, or better jobs, raise their income levels, provide better educational opportunities, and renovate and revitalize the communities that minorities live in, not just African Americans but Hispanics as well, I believe a lot of the crime and a lot of the disenfranchisement that they're experiencing would be solved."

"Well, what makes you think you can fix this?"

That was Trump's sweet spot. "Who's a better builder than Donald Trump?"

What about jobs?

He said, "If you cut me, I bleed jobs."

What about education?

"I support school choice."

Okay then. We were very satisfied with his answers.

* * *

I found it remarkable that on that day, in that room, Trump adopted a position of humility. It seemed to me then, as well as now, that he has an old-school 1950s-like reverence for clergy. When he came into that room, he immediately adopted the position of the lesser and acknowledged the clergy as the greater. He humbled himself in our sight. He said, "While you guys were pursuing a higher calling, I was out building buildings. I think it's time for me to catch up."

This let me know that he honestly felt that what we did as preachers was much more important than what he did as a developer. And it also gave me insight into his mindset.

Younger people think about their destiny. Older people think about their legacy. Apparently there was still a void in Trump's spirit, a lack of fulfillment that could only be satisfied through public service on the highest level. I also think that at this juncture of his life, he was wondering about the afterlife. He believes in heaven and hell, and undoubtedly wants to make heaven his eternal resting place.

He again requested that we pray on him and pray for him, which we did.

This time, however, a lot of the pastors pulled their cell phones out. What should have been a private, solemn moment became a social media event. Some were grandstanding, trying to lay hands on him and attempting to "slay him in the spirit" on the floor or something. He wasn't familiar with that. Some tried to lay a hand on his forehead, reaching under his hair, and he was taken aback a bit. They were trying to maximize that moment. There was a somewhat puzzled look on Trump's face, but he was enduring it.

After the prayer, we sat back down and the conversation continued. A lot of the preachers were excessively complimentary. They began comparing Trump to King Cyrus in the Bible, who was raised up to liberate the people of God. One preacher even compared him to John the Baptist. When he said that, I leaned over to Trump, whom I was sitting next to, and said, "So now you're John the Baptist, huh?" He leaned over to me and said, "I've been called a lot of things in my life, but I've never been called John the Baptist before." We both laughed. Everyone was wondering what we were laughing about. It was our private joke.

After a while, some of the preachers insisted that Trump change his style. They asked him to stop being so confrontational and combative, and said that if he would change, they would pray about and consider voting for him.

As preacher after preacher stated what they believed Trump should change, others became empowered to speak up, until it became a room full of critics pointing out what they perceived Trump's flaws to be and what he needed to fix. It went on like that for quite some time. At some suggestions he nodded slightly, but for the most part, he just sat there and took it.

Trump is one of the best listeners I've ever met. While he's listening, he's processing.

At one point, he said, "I'm a counterpuncher. I rarely hit first, but I always hit back," and the preachers replied, "Well, stop hitting back so hard and so much. Stop responding sometimes." I watched them take advantage of the situation. They seemed to have him on the ropes, and his respect for clergy restrained him from commenting the way that he could or should have.

After a while, I couldn't take it anymore. I actually had begun to feel sorry for him over the way they were ganging up on him. I don't like bullies, and they were trying to bully Trump. So I spoke up, because I knew they wouldn't challenge me the way they were challenging him. "Don't tone down anything!" I insisted.

Trump seemed startled. "What?"

The preachers were surprised, but nobody said anything.

The reason I don't like bullies is because I used to be one in my former life, to my regret. I remember once, when my wife and I preached at a citywide anti-drug crusade, there was an altar call for people to give their lives to Jesus. The first person in that line was a guy who, when I last saw him years ago...I was stomping him in his face. My heart smote me when I saw him in that line. I was too ashamed to pray for him. I had to ask my wife to do it. I had to tell him I was sorry about what I had done to him in the past, and asked him to forgive me, which he did. I regret the bully in my past.

I explained to Trump what I thought his appeal was. "The thing that I like about you, and if America sees it...if they see out there what I see back here, is your authenticity. You be you. Don't let these guys..." and I waved my hand at the preachers.

They didn't like it, but they knew better than to speak up.

"Don't let these guys take you out of your personality. America doesn't want a watered-down, fake version of Donald Trump. Don't go out there and pretend to be somebody that you're not. You just be you."

Trump got the message. "Oh, you think... You think I should continue being the way I am?"

"Yep."

"That's interesting," Trump said, still processing.

The other black preachers in the room reinforced my view. "Keep that!" one said. "Keep doing you."

Soon, nearly all of the black preachers in the room rallied in support, urging Trump on.

People don't say it now, but before he ran for president, Trump had tapped into the black community by being a big, bold personality. He is partly a product of the black community, a hip-hop icon. Trump is cited on more than twenty rap records, on which the artists rap about being like him: the bling, the money, the swag, the bravado, the chutzpah, and the luxury. All that is a part of the hip-hop culture; it's part of the presentation. You see it in the videos and the performances.

Later, I told Trump that if he wanted to win black votes, he would have to be his own man. He couldn't be another stereotypical politician with empty promises. We like leaders with courage. Leaders who are fearless. Leaders with balls.

One thing I noticed about Democrats was that they gave black people only emotional reasons, not rational ones, to oppose Trump. They didn't tell us, "Don't vote for Trump because of the economy." They didn't tell us, "Don't vote for Trump because of tariffs." Instead they said, "Trump hates you; he is a racist." They said the same to Hispanics. They told women he hates women, that he's sexist and wants to go back to the 1950s. They never gave reasons related to national security, foreign relations, the economy, jobs, or the performance of 401(k) plans.

Pretty soon, the black preachers began to dominate the conversation, and the white evangelicals felt a bit left out. Sensing this, I told Trump, "Wait a minute. I'll tell you what. We need to have our own all-black meeting with you."

Trump loved the idea. "Yes, we need to have a meeting where we can discuss things relevant and pertinent to the black community. I'll tell you what. I'll be down in Georgia next week. I have a rally down there next Friday. You guys meet me down there, and we can discuss it. Bring as many African-American people as you want."

That's not the kind of thing a racist would say.

During the meeting, I kept getting texts from Cohen saying: "Say something about me to the boss. Tell the boss that Michael's doing a good job for him." I instantly saw that Cohen craved affirmation from Trump. It was a personal foible that would later impact his life and make many people around him suffer. But that was in the future. At the moment, it just seemed a strange thing for him to be thinking about during that historic meeting.

* * *

When we got to the Georgia rally, I saw the Tea Party activist Herman Cain there. I knew who he was, how he had thrown his hat in the presidential ring before and how the left had done a hatchet job on him. I respected him highly and was excited to meet him. He was very warm and engaging then, as he is now. Presently, one of the event coordinators came over to me and said, "Pastor Scott, can you open it up with a prayer?"

It caught me off guard, but I stood before the thousands and prayed. Then I gave a brief exhortation. Cain came up a little while after me; he was there with Trump from day one.

At Trump's very first rally, two black people had been asked to speak.

The crowd was 98 percent white, but I sensed no racism in that arena. Those people from Georgia seemed happy to listen to a black preacher with a Northern accent.

Trump arrived late. Trump Force One had a mechanical problem, and he had to take his second plane, the smaller one. As a result, he wasn't able to give us black preachers the time that he had promised us. We engaged for around fifteen minutes. He said, "Look, why don't we do this? If you don't mind, let's meet next week at Trump Tower. I'll be there. Come on back up. Bring as many as you want to and come on. We'll be able to meet without any interruptions." Then the organizers came and asked him to go onstage.

I met Trump's daughter Tiffany for the first time there. She was just a nice, quiet young lady standing by. I didn't know she was his daughter. I thought she was a campaign worker. She spoke to me and was very friendly.

Trump did his thing at the rally. Afterward, there was a news conference. He invited me and the other preachers onstage with him.

He handed me the microphone. I found some words. "The American system of government is divided into three branches. You've got the executive branch, the legislative branch, and the judicial branch. As a legislator, I don't know what kind of legislator Donald Trump would be. As a judicator, I don't know what kind of judicator he would be. But as a chief executive, I've got belief in him right there. That's the job for him.

To me, he's America's CEO; I can see him as being the CEO of this company called America."

I meant it. If I didn't, I wouldn't have said it.

* * *

Exactly 108 preachers, mostly black, showed up at Trump Tower the following week. The media was out in front of Trump Tower, and a few of us addressed them on the way in, but there were not a lot of reporters at that particular time, and they didn't know who was going in and out of the Tower for what. Many more preachers had been invited, but they were intimidated when they began receiving phone calls and texts. Someone had put out fake news that they were meeting with Trump to endorse him, which was not true, and a lot of the preachers got spooked. The notion that black leaders would even meet with Trump, who was running on the Republican platform, was considered heresy, at least to the press. Democratic preachers who had *not* been invited began to pound their soapbox in order to intimidate others, and they succeeded with many.

Other preachers called and began to make excuses when the controversy heated up. They were flat-out scared. At first they had been excited to meet with him, but then a number of them chickened out.

But 108 preachers and black Christian leaders, according to the Secret Service's count, did attend the meeting. I was surprised to meet Omarosa—most famously known as a contestant on the first season of *The Apprentice*—there for the very first time. I knew who she was from television, and that she was an ordained minister. She and I became friends immediately. She was from Youngstown, Ohio, and I was from Cleveland, so there was an instant Ohio connection. I think she was there at the invitation of Michael Cohen, or she had found out about the meeting and been determined to attend. Regardless of the reason, she was there and was an unabashed Trump supporter.

We opened up the meeting with prayer. I gave an introductory speech, and contrary to the Democrats' party line, there weren't any

Uncle Toms in that room. There wasn't anybody up there trying to shine Trump's shoes or kiss up to him. He got a lot of hard questions.

You would have thought that Trump was on the witness stand and we were the prosecution.

I intentionally allowed really tough questions as I coordinated the meeting. "What do you think about black people getting killed by the police?" "What about these allegations of racism against you?" "Do you like or don't like black people?" "Are you a racist?" "What about Eric Garner, who was killed in a chokehold?" "What about Trayvon Martin?"

No question was off-limits. We went around the room, with everyone asking questions. Some of the questions stood out. One pastor asked, "What's this stuff about the guy that got kind of roughed up at your rally? You had your people take him out."

Trump's response was perfect. "At your church, if you're in the middle of preaching, and a guy gets up and starts to disrupt your service, what would happen?"

"Oh, my security would take him out of there."

"Well, alright then. What do you want me to do? You answered your own question."

The pastor considered Trump's comment. "Yeah, you're right. Okay."

Every question they asked, he answered without blinking. He didn't duck. He didn't dodge. He didn't deflect. We had a wonderful time. There was a lot of back-and-forth, a lot of intensity, humor, insight, combativeness, confrontation, and great discussion. We aired it out!

The pastors in that room made me proud of the way they represented themselves, Christianity, the black community, and America at large. I was impressed with their knowledge of the issues, and their comments and suggestions regarding how to solve some of the problems that plague all of America...not just black America. The meeting wrapped up with my saying, "Does anybody else have anything to say to him?"

Everybody said, "No, we're good."

"How many of you dislike Donald Trump?" I asked. Not one person raised their hand.

I pressed on. "If Donald Trump pulled out his checkbook and offered to write a check to everybody in here, who wouldn't take the money?" No one put up their hand.

"Let's go downstairs as a consensus and make a joint statement. We will say that we had a great dialogue, a great talk. We covered a lot of bases."

There was a buzz of agreement.

Then I moved to a conclusion. "We have pledge cards for those of you who want to endorse Trump." We passed out the cards. "If you're interested and want to endorse him right now, you can. If not, take it with you or leave it here. Nobody is pressuring you."

About half of the people signed cards, but their signatures wouldn't match their actions a few minutes later.

I nominated a friend of mine, Cindy Trimm, whom I had known for years, as our spokesperson. I didn't want to do it myself, because my relationship with and favor of Donald Trump had begun to be known, and I didn't think a statement by me would have as much impact as one by Cindy.

She actually represented a number of things that the media said Trump was opposed to. She was an immigrant (legal), black, and a woman. That covered three bases right there. Her support contradicted charges of Trump's xenophobia, racism, and sexism in one fell swoop.

We all discussed what we were going to say when we got downstairs, with different preachers making different suggestions, until we came to an agreement. After the meeting formally concluded with a word of prayer, it took Trump nearly an hour to get from the far end of the conference room, where he and I had been seated at the head of the conference table, to the door. Everyone wanted a selfie, an autograph, a handshake, a hug, a brief conversation; and he indulged every single person there. He was nice and hospitable to everyone in that room, and it wasn't fake. He and they were having a good time eating and laughing and joking and hanging out. He was in no rush to leave. Finally I said, "We have to go downstairs now. The media's been waiting for hours."

When the elevator doors opened into the marble lobby of Trump Tower, the lights from the network cameras were blinding. Scores of media people were there from all the major networks, unlike anything any of these preachers had ever experienced, including myself. They were pushing and shoving and shouting questions and taking pictures, and the preachers got frightened. They cut and ran! I watched some turn their collars up and pull their hats down and go the other way, blending in with the crowd. People who were with us upstairs disappeared when we got downstairs. So much for consensus. So much for the joint statement and those pledges that they had signed. Something changed in Cindy as well. She said everything except what we had talked about upstairs. She went off script. She seemed like a deer in the headlights.

The media was shouting questions and not letting her finish one answer before she had to tackle another question. They were acting more like Democratic Party enforcers than genuine journalists.

At that point I took the microphone out of her hand. I couldn't let her continue. I looked around. Almost all of the 108 black preachers had melted away. Vanished. Only a few remained.

One thing I'll say about my colleagues, black and white, is this: It's easy to talk tough. It's easy to be bold and commanding when you're in a pulpit with a captive audience, with security and deacons and elders who support you and hang on your every word. It's easy to talk about all the power and authority you possess as a believer in friendly surroundings, when you're in charge and everyone is at your beck and call. But when you're faced with a hostile media looking to stone you, when you have to take a stand for what you believe outside the church walls— that's when you find out how much power, authority, and courage you really possess. That's when you find out if you're a real leader or simply a manager—if you're fearless or fearful.

"You like Donald Trump?" one reporter shouted.

"Yes, I like him," I answered.

"So, you're endorsing him?" demanded another.

"Yes, I'm endorsing him."

There. I had said it. On national television. I was on the Trump train, no matter what happened. Still, I had no idea how bumpy that ride would be.

* * *

Later, one preacher told me, "My son loves Donald Trump, and I like him, too. I like what he's talking about, and I'm going to vote for him, but I'm not telling anybody." And there are many more black people like that. I coined a term for them. I call them the "Incog-Negroes." There are a number of black people who like Trump, but they don't want to argue about it at work, or with family, or in their communities. They keep their opinions private, but when they're in the voting booth, they vote for Trump.

But that's not me. I am not a halfway friend. I am not a lukewarm ally. I'm ride or die. If I am in, I am all the way in.

The next few weeks would test my resolve. A whole lot of people were about to turn against me.

TWO

The next day, my social media was flooded. "You coon." "You Uncle Tom." "You boot-licker." "You sellout."

I've always been a stand-up guy. Anybody who knows me knows that I'm no coon or Uncle Tom; I have civil rights awards from the NAACP. In fact, I intentionally was hard on Trump in our private meetings. But the public saw only the press conference, not the discussion in the conference room.

I'm disappointed by the colleagues who didn't defend me—my comrades in the Black Church who had known me for decades. They know that I've never had any scandal attached to my name. I've been with the same woman for forty years. I have zero babies out of wedlock. I haven't had a drink of liquor in forty years. I haven't used a drug or smoked marijuana in forty years. I haven't smoked a cigarette in forty years. I haven't defrauded any of my church's members. I've never resorted to selling or to using gimmicks. I haven't made any false prophecies. I haven't preached any false doctrines or gotten caught up in any fads. There just hasn't been any scandal attached to me or my church.

Yet they wouldn't stand with me.

They didn't have to agree with me on Trump. All they had to do was attest to the truth, that the hateful things being said about me just weren't true.

"Disappointed" doesn't even describe how I really felt. "Pissed off" is more like it. It was all I could do not to retaliate when my colleagues began attacking me for my choice, all I could do to not go "scorched earth" and tear the covers off a lot of the black preachers. The only reason I didn't was because the Church world was watching, the innocents in the pews, and I didn't want to tarnish the Church in any way.

I remember the scandals that rocked the Church in the eighties, and how the preachers fought one another in public while the world watched and laughed. It was hard for me, because I know where the bodies are buried. I've pastored my church for more than twenty-five years and have been a Christian for nearly forty years.

I know all the secrets of my colleagues, both big and small. I know about the good ol' boys' clubs. I know which black preachers still abuse drugs, which ones are closet alcoholics, which ones have babies out of wedlock, which ones are sleeping with as many women as they can, which ones are gay, which ones are lesbians, which ones are thieves, liars, and false prophets. There are a number of open secrets in the Black Church, and I know most of them. What was especially irritating after I came out in support of Trump on national TV is the fact that a lot of the preachers who were criticizing me for supporting Trump are some of the worst offenders—the biggest whoremongers, the biggest hypocrites in the Church world today!

My personal battle was in not exposing them all. I wasn't afraid to name names, either.

Had it not been for God and my wife, I would have put them all on blast!

Truth be told, I saw a big opportunity for the black community: a direct line to the White House. No other candidate has sat in the room with black preachers and said, "You've got an open door at the White House if I get in." This was what we'd been waiting for since the end of the Civil War—an open invitation to 1600 Pennsylvania Avenue. *Come on! Let's go!* I thought. *What do we have to lose?*

We were getting a chance to get what we had always wanted: a president working in cooperation with the black community. Trump told everybody in that room in Trump Tower that day that they could "come up here and see me anytime you want to." To me, the black preachers who didn't support him were being stupid. They missed their shot. They let fear and a lack of courage prevent them from taking advantage of a golden opportunity to benefit the Black Church, the black community, and all of America.

I felt like Noah begging people to come onto the ark. They didn't want to come. Too afraid of the media. Too afraid of social media. Too afraid of people's opinions. It shows me that they do not believe what they preach or have the faith in God that they profess to have. They have more faith in themselves and people than they have in God. They don't see God as the source of their supply. They see people as their source. They're afraid to lose the money. They fear people leaving their church more than they fear displeasing God. Many of them have called me since then and said, "I didn't see it. I should have stayed in. Is it too late?"

"No," I've told them, "it's not too late. I'll invite you to some things, but you'll never have the relationship with him that you could have had."

In fact, recently, when Trump had some preachers up to the White House, one of them said, "Well, Mr. President, you have a relationship with Pastor Scott. But we don't have that relationship, and we want that type of relationship with you, too."

Trump looked at him and said, "He earned that."

It's easy to come along and say that you want a relationship with the president once he is president, but everyone—including Trump—knows that you didn't want that relationship when he was number seventeen in a field of seventeen candidates.

All that criticism just steeled my resolve, throwing gasoline on a fire. It made me dig my heels in deeper. *Oh, I'm a coon? Oh, you think you're going to bully me out of supporting this guy? Not gonna happen.*

After the black preachers meeting in Trump Tower, which was on a Friday, I went home on Saturday and went to my church on Sunday. A crowd of reporters was waiting outside.

"Can we get a statement about the meeting at Trump Tower?"

"You stick around for the service, and I'll give you a statement at the end of the message," I responded.

They could sit in the church and hear my sermon like everyone else. I preached from the twenty-seventh chapter of the Book of Acts, in which the apostle Paul is taken outside the city walls to be stoned to death for the crime of preaching the truth. Then God raised the apostle up from the dead, and Paul, rather than run away, went right back into the city and started preaching the same message again.

Then I added these words for the men and women of the media: "For those of you that are waiting for my statement, here it is: I'll go up there again, and next time, I'll take two hundred preachers instead of one hundred."

Their mouths gaped, and the congregation went crazy. Everybody started clapping. Everyone except the reporters.

* * *

My stubborn support for Trump was partly the result of my personal experience with Barack Obama and his campaign. I didn't like Obama playing the "black card" during his run for president in 2008, especially because he had as much white support as black support.

Back then, I went on my gospel radio station in Cleveland and said, "If the only reason you're voting for Obama is because he's black, you insulted him."

The phone lines lit up. I said, "I don't hire a landscaper just because he is black. I won't hire a plumber just because he's black. They need to be qualified. They need to be able to plumb. They better be able to cut grass. If the only qualification Obama has is that he's black, then you're saying that he's not qualified."

I always thought that voting for a guy because of his race was just as bad as voting against him because of his race.

I had the opportunity to meet then Senator Obama in 2006.

U.S. Senator Sherrod Brown (an Ohio Democrat) with his wife, Connie Schultz, a Pulitzer Prize–winning reporter for the *Cleveland Plain Dealer*, had organized a political fundraiser. I allowed them to use my church and its banquet halls free of charge. They had all the bigwigs in the Democratic Party there, and nobody was complaining about separation of church and state.

They were bringing in this new hotshot senator named Barack Obama who had made his name at the Democratic Convention in 2004 when he hit the ball out of the park with his amazing speech.

Sherrod and Connie and I were in a space that we were using as a green room, having great conversation.

The door opened, and Obama came into the room. He recognized Senator Brown.

"Good to see you, Sherrod, Connie." He warmly greeted the senator and his wife.

Then he looked at me and said, "Hello. My pastor told me to tell you hi also."

I knew Jeremiah Wright probably hadn't said that, because he and I didn't know each other, but it was good for Obama to extend greetings on his behalf, which is common behavior in the Black Church. But then he gradually steered the conversation to include only the senator, his wife, and himself. I began feeling like a third wheel. It was subtly rude.

I try to be as hospitable as I can. Everyone that knows me knows I'm friendly, down to earth, and as humble as I can be—but I'm nobody's pushover. We were in my church. I had provided cheese, crackers, shrimp, dip, fruits, and meats. I was the host. There were four of us in the room, but pretty soon only three were included in the conversation. Obama had effectively cut me out, like I'm a little guy in a room of big guys.

After a while, the senator and his wife went out to talk to the crowd attending the event. I was alone with Obama, and our interaction was strained, to say the least. Here we were, two black leaders in the room together, but there was an uncomfortable silence in the air. I began to feel like a kid on a first date, because our "conversation" had devolved into a series of questions with one-word answers.

He would not engage with me the way he engaged with the others. I know they were colleagues, but we were still two black guys in the room together. The NBA playoffs were on at the time, but he didn't really have much to say about that.

I'm an engaging person, but I'm not a kiss-up. I don't care who you are; I'm not, as the Bible calls it, a "respecter of persons." I wasn't going to continue to try to make conversation with someone who obviously didn't want to talk.

If it had been Trump, we would have had great conversation, because Trump is a people person. He loves to hold court. He loves to engage. Obama was saving his words and energy for the people in the next room. *The hell with him*, I thought. *I'm not gonna sit in here and keep trying to hold conversation with someone who obviously doesn't want to talk.*

I did ask him, "Are you thinking about running for president in '08?"

He simply replied, "Well..." and that was it. He didn't have much of a "people" personality, at least in private, as far as I was concerned. He didn't try to interact. He's the only politician I ever met who was comfortable sitting in silence with someone who could potentially be a big supporter in a swing state, as Ohio was in 2008. I had a fairly large church and an influential radio station in Cleveland, Ohio's largest metro area. I could have been a big ally.

I try not to be judgmental. I engage with people for a living, and I interact with all types. I try to locate where people are and meet them there, on their own terms. As a pastor, I'm in the people business. I understand he could have had some reservations. I understand that he could have been having a difficult day, even though he had been a great conversationalist with Senator Brown and his wife. But he wasn't the cultural phenomenon then that he became later; he was still an up-and-coming freshman senator. If you are a public servant, then act like one. Don't act like an elitist. Serve the public, and at least be friendly.

Finally, after what seemed like an eternity of uncomfortable silence, I called one of my guys and said, "When he's ready to go in, walk him in." Then I left the room. I saw Obama one more time as he was leaving, and we shook hands goodbye.

Months later, his campaign came calling.

I allowed the Obama campaign to use my church and its facilities for a few events. Then staffers asked if they could have office space upstairs to use as local campaign headquarters. They wanted to use it rent-free, and I agreed.

They also said they didn't want to pay for utilities. The campaign was raising millions but didn't want to pay rent or utilities, and staffers wanted twenty-four-hour access to the building, which would require them having a key and the code to the alarm system. No deal, I said. Our church facility is a multipurpose building with banquet halls, a daycare center, a radio station, and a lot of office space for lease. We put millions of dollars into its renovation, because it's a historic landmark. We lock the doors at a certain time every night and put the alarm on. I was not going to give them twenty-four-hour access to our facility. No deal!

* * *

My wife and I were watching Obama give a speech on television one day, and she said to me, "He thinks he's the smartest guy in the room." He was proclaiming to be about hope and optimism, but I knew that he was describing a dream that was nearly impossible deliver on. At my age, I'm past the point of having rose-colored glasses on. I try to be a realist.

One demerit, at least as far as I was concerned, was the fact that Obama had never signed the front of a check. He had never been more than a community organizer. He had made his name and hit a home run during his speech at the 2004 Democratic Convention, and parlayed that into a U.S. Senate seat. I've got to give it to him; he's not a dumb guy.

He and his team executed their strategy to perfection and made history in the process. His PR people did a great job transforming Obama into a cultural phenomenon. He was handsome, articulate, educated, polished, a good husband, and a great father of two beautiful daughters. The total package.

If white America could be convinced to ignore the color of his skin, he might have a chance. His future vice president, Joe Biden, said that Obama was "the first mainstream African American who is articulate and bright and clean and a nice-looking guy." What kind of endorsement was that? "The first"?

Anyway, Obama became a cultural phenomenon, much like Michael Jackson, the Beatles, and Elvis Presley. Michael Jackson had just as many white fans as black ones. James Brown was a cultural phenomenon, as was Muhammad Ali. Obama was able to tap into that market. He had the same cross-cultural appeal.

Everybody was enamored with Obama. It was taboo to say anything bad about him. Actually, he was criticism-proof. If you were white and criticized him, you were branded a racist. If you were black and criticized him, you were branded a sellout and an Uncle Tom. Black women in particular fell in love with him, because to so many he represented their ideal black man: good husband of one wife, provider for his family. He represented the "black" American dream, and there was nothing wrong with that. Black people need heroes, too. We need icons, too. Everyone was enamored with and enthusiastic about Obama. Except me. I did not dislike him, but I wasn't captivated by the "Yes we can" mantra. I'm more of a "How can we?" guy.

Part of my immunity to Obama's "spell" was because I was from Cleveland. Cleveland had the first black big-city mayor, Carl Stokes. When I was a kid, Stokes was our hero. He was Obama before Obama: intelligent, articulate, handsome. Beautiful family. Young, optimistic. A product of our community who generated a tremendous amount of civic pride.

As mayor, he encountered his share of opposition, battling with the city council and the police department. The same party politics that are prevalent now were prevalent then. He was unable to change the landscape of the city, even though he tried to implement policies like "Cleveland, Now!" a program that was geared toward urban revitalization. He was also instrumental in providing job opportunities at city hall for black people, jobs that previously had been unavailable to them.

Stokes served two terms as mayor and decided not to run for reelection. Upon leaving Cleveland, he went on the college lecture circuit, then became the first black television anchorman in New York City before returning to Cleveland to serve as a judge in municipal court. He's remembered more for being the first black mayor than for his mayoral accomplishments.

So I saw Obama through my experiences with Cleveland, my hometown, the site of the first black mayor.

* * *

I've always voted for the person rather than for the party. I voted for Ronald Reagan twice. I voted for George H. W. Bush once.

I liked Bill Clinton a lot. He was a very brilliant, charismatic man. A childhood friend whose family was originally from Arkansas knew him and worked with him, eventually taking a job in his administration, so I voted for Clinton. I voted for George W. Bush over Al Gore. In 2008, it almost came down to a coin flip between Obama and John McCain. I would argue at the barbershop for McCain—because, I said, if I closed my eyes and listened to them both, I would vote for McCain. The guys in the barbershop weren't having it. They all said McCain was a racist—the same thing they had said about George H. W. and George W. Bush, and Reagan. I remember hearing in the community in the eighties, "Don't vote Reagan. He's gonna cut welfare."

I had a problem with that statement then, as I still do now. It's as if welfare is the lifeline of the black community, that it's the only option most of us have. That without welfare we would not be able to survive as a people.

I was unfamiliar with that mindset. Growing up, we were never on welfare. My father always had a nice blue-collar job. He was able to buy a new car every four years, and would give my brother and me his old cars.

He helped me get my first job when I was fourteen years old, for fifty-three dollars a week, at a restaurant/grocery store in the inner city. The welfare mentality was foreign to me.

I didn't make the final decision as to whom I would vote for in 2008 until I got in the voting booth. I still remembered my interaction with Obama and his campaign, and to be honest, I just didn't particularly care for him. He seemed like an elitist to me. He didn't, as Ben Carson would say years later, have a "real" black experience, having been raised by his white mother and grandmother in Hawaii. He came off as being "cool," but it wasn't all the way legit. Whatever "street cred" he had was given to him by the hip-hop community.

I wanted him to be a good president more than just a black president. The black on top of the good would be icing on the cake, but my priority was a good president.

But I'm still black. Regardless of what goes on, our blackness connects us. I say that to this day, that whatever side of the political aisle we're on, whatever our ideas and opinions are, blackness still connects us. There's a commonality in blackness that connects African Americans all over this country. You can't put it into words, but all black people know what it is. It's better "felt than telt."

It's like the word "cool" for blacks. You can't put "cool" into words, but you know it when you see it. You understand what being "cool" is. It extends to our racial perceptions as blacks, as well. We have racism detectors built into our psyche. We can see it and know it whether it's subtle or overt. We can see it in the little things as well as the big. I've always said that racism is like ugliness: I can't describe it fully, but I know it when I see it. It comes across in looks, in comments, in interactions. It comes across in things as small as a cashier trying not to touch your hand when giving you your change at the store. It comes across in the way a waitress serves you and serves the white people at the table next to you. Racism does not usually show its ugly head in big ways, like it once did. It now shows up in little ways.

In the end, in 2008, I voted for Obama.

I supported him openly. In fact, I was the first black pastor in Cleveland to publicly support him. Most of the other black pastors supported and endorsed Hillary Clinton at that time. One current Democratic city councilman told me that it was my support of Obama that convinced him to support him; that if it had not been for me, he would have stayed with Hillary.

Internally, I was still harboring doubts about Obama, but when I got into the voting booth, I let our blackness connect us. Obama was proclaiming hope and dreams. I decided to give him a chance.

* * *

After Obama won the 2008 presidential election, a lot of black people had mistaken notions. They thought that once Obama was president, we would get to move to the front of the bus, and the white folks were going to move to the back of the bus. We would be able to take our place in this society that we helped build, finally gaining the upper hand. Some thought that a blanket of black utopia would descend upon America. After all, we had a black president now. But the black utopia never came.

Good things would have to come through hard work. Not through magic. Or elections. I had been invited to and attended George W. Bush's inauguration. I did not receive an invitation to attend Obama's.

THREE

I was born into a pretty average family on a street named Tuscora in Cleveland's inner city. But my father made sure that my mother, my brother, my sister, and I didn't stay there forever.

As I mentioned, my father always had a job and we were never on welfare. He was working at the post office when I was born. Then he drove a bus for the Cleveland Transit System. Then he got a job at the *Cleveland Press* as a teamster. Then he worked for the water company. He had a very strong work ethic, which I believe he passed down to me. He didn't make my mother work. If and when she did work jobs, it was because she wanted to, not because she had to, and whatever money she made was hers to keep.

When I was six years old, my parents moved us to Cleveland's Lee-Harvard neighborhood.

At the time, I did not realize the significance of what my parents had done. I just knew that friends and relatives began acting a little funny. They would say, "Oh, you think you're something that you're living over there now." But what did I know? I was a kid.

It was a monumental thing they did back then, moving us into that solidly middle-class, predominantly white neighborhood. We drove out of the inner city into what was one of the more affluent areas for black people in 1965. It was less than one year after the passage of the Civil

Rights Act. We helped integrate our street. We were maybe the second or third black family on the street.

I grew up playing with white and black kids; color was never an issue for us. Maybe that's what makes it easy for me to walk in this Republican world now. Then the "white flight" occurred in the 1970s, and the neighborhood became all black. By the end of the 1980s, it was as bad as the inner city. But when I was kid, it was clean and comparatively affluent. Safe. Diverse. Every father had a job and mowed the lawn and took care of his home on Saturdays. Most of the blacks on the street were first-time homeowners and had a lot of pride in their property.

I did not grow up in a "hate whitey" home. My father believed in hard work: get up, get a job, go to work. He instilled that work ethic in us. He did not blame the white man for any problems that we had. Anything that we had or didn't have was because of work. He never walked around the house saying, "I hate them white folks" or "Them white folks this, them white folks that..." He didn't put that mentality in our heads.

I'm not knocking anybody else's story. I'm not knocking anybody else's truth. Maybe some were raised in the South, maybe some did have crosses burned on their grass...but they didn't burn them on ours. We weren't raised in that climate. When the riots began in the mid-sixties, my father didn't harp on it as if the white man was oppressing the blacks. My father said, "Get a job, go to work, and make your own way." That's the way it was.

When we first arrived in Lee-Harvard, I was in for two surprises: the houses looked new (they were barely ten years old), and there were a lot of white kids—Italians, Poles, Germans, Czechs, and others—living there.

We didn't encounter any racism that we were aware of. I don't know what parents were telling their children at home when the doors were closed, but we played with all the kids in the neighborhood: baseball, football, basketball, kickball, hide-and-go-seek, tag. We were in and out of one another's houses.

My father had black friends and white friends. He was a very good baseball player who played in fast-pitch baseball leagues and won several batting titles. He would take us with him. On the baseball team, there were blacks and whites.

This just shows you how fast America was changing. A decade and a half earlier, Jackie Robinson had shocked the world by becoming the first black ballplayer in Major League Baseball. Then, fifteen years later, black and white American kids were playing baseball together like it had always been that way.

* * *

Growing up, our home was not perfect. My parents argued, cussed, and fussed. It got violent sometimes. My mother and father were two young people with the same issues that many other couples had, and we did like many black families do even now. We kept our family business in the family.

My mother was no milquetoast. She gave as well as she got. She was very quiet up to her breaking point, but when she exploded, she could peel the paper off the walls with her tongue.

In flashes of memory of those days, I remember being used to my father coming home at a certain time every night. I remember the first couple of times on a Friday night that Daddy didn't get home at 7 p.m. We kids were worried—is Daddy alright?—and my mother would be pissed off. She knew what we didn't. Then we would go to sleep and wake up and he would be there, and there would be an argument. But we didn't connect the dots. We were kids. This was home.

Looking back, I try not to view my parents through a child's eyes, which is something I think too many adults do. Once I grew up and got married and had children and grandchildren, I gained a new perspective on some of the things I had been hard on my parents about. I can now think of my parents in terms of being a husband and a wife, rather than just a mother and a father. In spite of the volatility of their marriage, my father and mother stayed married for forty-six years, until the day she died of pancreatic cancer. He never walked out on her, and he never abandoned me and my two brothers and two sisters. He still owns that same house he bought in 1965, and he never remarried.

My parents drank socially and on weekends. You can't go to work every day or raise five kids while overindulging. There was liquor around the house. My father and mother both smoked cigarettes; sometimes he smoked a little reefer, too—not too much, not all the time. One day in 1966, my father walked into the house and said, "I'm not smoking cigarettes anymore." He never smoked again. I found it amazing that he had that kind of discipline. He would come in and say sometimes, "My belly is looking too big. I'm not gonna drink beer for a while," and then he wouldn't drink beer for months, until his belly went down.

I see a lot of him in me. He was very outspoken, loud when he wanted to be, courageous when he had to be, and seemed utterly fearless to us kids. He and my mother were both avid readers, especially of black literature, and they passed that reading habit down to us kids. We had only one television in the house, so we had to read books for escapism and enjoyment. My mother bought a ten-volume set of Bibles for us for Christmas in 1965, and we devoured them. They provided a foundation for my life then that I continue to stand upon now.

* * *

When I was in first grade, the school recommended that my parents take me to a psychiatrist to take an intelligence test. My scores surprised all of the adults. With a thrill in her voice, the psychiatrist told me: "You can be anything that you want to be when you grow up."

After that test, I was transferred to another school. I was sent across town to what was called a "major work" class, where the smart kids were. Today they might call it a gifted and talented program.

I was in there with the smart kids. But I wasn't one of the good kids.

* * *

When I was in second grade, the teacher taped my mouth shut in French class. In fifth grade, I had to sit in the coatroom for the whole year. Then when sixth grade rolled around and I had the same French teacher, she said, "You know where your spot is; get in there."

I was one of the more mischievous kids in class. One of the class cut-ups. A class clown. An attention seeker. A sixth-grade teacher once got upset with me and chewed me out in front of the class. Then she finished by yelling, "And you have the highest IQ of every student in here!"

Looking back on it, I know now that teachers shouldn't have been able to get away with that kind of stuff. It would be called abuse or shaming today. It didn't bother me, though. I'm glad they didn't have medication back then, because they probably would have tried to put me on Ritalin or something.

In junior high, we had to ride to school across town in one of those yellow buses, and we would get teased. The other kids thought that because we were in that class with the smart kids, we were little punks or something. I wasn't anybody's punk.

In my neighborhood, the white kids moved out, and the black kids started moving in. The black families that moved in all came from the inner city, and some from the projects. I gravitated toward a certain type of friend, to the "bad kids." The cigarette smokers. The cussers. The young hoodlums.

My friends and I smoked cigarettes and stole bikes, painting and selling them. We broke into houses. We stole from stores. We were the kids that parents didn't want their kids to play with.

When I was in the sixth grade, my friend Terry asked me a question that I didn't understand: "Do you want to cut today?"

"What's that?"

"Cut."

"What does that mean?"

"Meaning we skip school today. We don't..."

I got it. "Let's do it."

We skipped that morning, hung out at a gas station. Then that afternoon, we went to school, and we were the big shots. We had cut class. Terry and I both lived in a neighborhood where—even though our school friends were the smart kids, and most of them were good kids—we hung out with the bad kids. With the reefer smokers, the cigarette smokers, and the wine drinkers.

I remember the very first time my brother and a friend and I smoked reefer. An older guy liked my older sister. My brother and I were hanging around, "protecting" our sister. He wanted to get rid of us, so he gave us a joint. I didn't know what it was. But my brother knew, and our best friend, Ken, knew. We went over to Ken's garage to smoke it. I was scared. I was like, "How do you do it? What are you supposed to do?" They lit it, and then we smoked it. We put our hands over our mouths, held our breaths, and that was the first time we did it. It was cool. I think that I faked it, like I was higher than I really was.

Terry and I, along with our entire class, then got sent to Alexander Hamilton Junior High School, way across town, because it had a "major work" program there. It was in a rougher neighborhood. The kids there were harder than the kids at the elementary school we had attended. You couldn't be soft in that hard environment, or they would make a punk out of you. They would take your money, smack you around, beat you up, and shake you down if you let them.

I once again gravitated to the "bad kids." The hoodlums. We got into fights, cut class, got into trouble, got suspended a lot, and did all the things that "bad kids" do. I remember once my father got called into the school because I was in trouble again. The principal told him that I was the ringleader of the troublemakers. I went home scared that I was gonna "get it" from my father, but when we went home and he told my mother what the principal had said, I heard him say, "He said that Darrell was the leader," with pride in his voice. He told me to cut all that crap out, but he was glad that I was a leader and not a follower.

Eventually, I got kicked out of Hamilton and sent to another junior high that was in our neighborhood. I was able to go to school with my brother and my neighborhood friends for the first time since the third grade, because all the "gifted students" went to school out of the neighborhood.

Now it was really "on." We drank wine and beer every single day. We smoked weed, took pills, cut class, and did every bad thing we could get away with.

It was the beginning of the "blaxploitation" era in Hollywood, and we all wanted to be just like "Superfly," with all of the trappings—the clothes, cars, and girls. Or "The Mack." Those cats were hip and cool. Drug dealers and pimps. They were our new heroes. They would "stick it to the Man," who was embodied by the police or the white establishment. They were what we all wanted to be.

We were coming out of the riots and oppression of the sixties, the struggle for civil rights. We were the new generation. We had been emboldened by the struggles of the sixties. James Brown sang our new anthem: "Say it loud, I'm black and I'm proud." We were loud, black, and proud. The blaxploitation heroes presented to us onscreen were the epitome of black pride to us. They were our role models.

Did Hollywood know or care about the impact those movies had on our culture? It was a very negative, very criminal image of successful blacks being presented to us. A lot of black kids wound up in the penitentiary or strung out on drugs or whatever from those movies, because those were the only heroes we had. Those movies were the only way at the time for us blacks to see ourselves in positions of power onscreen, in positions of authority and strength—not as janitors or porters or butlers or chauffeurs. We had an occasional black, like Bill Cosby in *I Spy*, but he was nonthreatening to white America. He also had to be paired with a white guy. We had Diahann Carroll as a single mom who was a nurse, but she was harmless and inoffensive. These new heroes, however, were rough. They didn't take whitey's crap. They stood up for themselves. They gave us the mindset of "sticking it to the Man," and that's what we wanted to do.

I, like so many others, got my hair done like Superfly. It was down past my shoulders. We had all the Superfly hats and stuff. In order to get this stuff, we needed money. If we wanted to get it, we had to get out there and get our own money. We had to have a job or a hustle. Without a job, the only way was to steal or sell drugs, because we wanted a lifestyle that our parents wouldn't support.

Every day we drank liquor. Every day we smoked weed. We would always supplement that with some other type of drug. Acid. Black Beauties, Red Devils, chocolate mescaline, blue mescaline, Orange Sunshine...whatever, you name it. We did that on top of cocaine, heroin. We didn't shoot it, we'd snort it. That was the lifestyle. That was the culture.

I remember the first encounter I had with the police. I was in Warrensville Heights, a nearby suburb, to shoplift at Value City. We were stealing and selling Knicker boots, which were "in" at that time. We'd go in the store with a pocketful of dirt and mud, try the boots on, reach in our pockets and rub the mud on the boots, and walk out of the store. The boots cost maybe forty-five or fifty dollars, and on the street we could sell them for fifteen to twenty-five dollars.

After we left the store with the boots, we went past a nearby drive-in and spotted a 1962 Thunderbird in the parking lot. The 1962 Thunderbird is 17.08 feet long. One of the true land yachts. We saw that it had been left overnight at the drive-in and that it had been stolen.

Our curiosity got the best of us. We tried to get it started.

I guess someone inside the drive-in saw us and called the police.

The cops were on us in seconds. "What are you kids doing here? Get over here. Put your hands on the car."

Another police car pulled in, and another officer got out. "What's going on? What did they do?"

I turned around. "We didn't do nothing."

The second cop knocked the hell out of me, saying, "Get your ass up against that car." He scuffed me around a bit.

They cuffed my brother and my friend. They had to put steel bands around my wrists because they ran out of handcuffs. There were two cops, two cuffs, and three of us.

At that time, black boys getting killed by police was a reality. Some killed black men back then, the same way some kill black men now.

The police drove us back up through some woods on a street called Emery Road. There are houses on that street now, but it was mostly woods back then.

I looked at my brother and mouthed the words, "They're going to kill us."

My brother said, "They might." In the seventies, we knew that the real possibility always existed of getting killed by white cops.

We all knew about a classmate of ours named Zach, who was a car thief. One Friday night he was arrested and never returned. By Monday, the talk was all over the school: "Zach killed himself in jail." Everyone knew that Zach didn't kill himself. Zach wasn't the type to kill himself over a stolen car. But he was a loudmouth. He must have mouthed off to the police. We knew that they had killed him.

In the 1970s, if you got caught by certain cops and you mouthed off or gave them a hard time, they were liable to kill you. I was arrested several times for different stuff after that, but I never mouthed off again. Instead of talking, I just planned my strategy: "What am I going to say? How am I going to get out of this?"

I didn't go to jail a lot, because I wasn't stupid. I didn't do dumb capers. I had enough sense to say, "I'm going to pass on that one."

I can look back on some of my experiences and see the hand of God in them. One time my friends and I stole a Cadillac on a Friday night. Now, one thing I didn't do was joyride in stolen cars. I would get it, go somewhere to strip it down, get rid of it, and be done with it. You drop the shell off; you don't joyride in it.

That Friday night, my friends had other ideas: "Let's strip it tomorrow; we want to ride tonight."

I wasn't having it. "I'm not riding around in a stolen car! Let me out here on the block in front of the beverage store."

My friend Terry and I got out.

He and I went into the store, bought some liquor, exchanged pleasantries, and left. We looked down the street and saw police lights strobing. We walked down there and saw our friends up against the car in cuffs. We had gotten out just in time. They had made it one block before getting busted. I look back on stuff like that and believe that was God preserving me.

* * *

In my circle, some guys were strictly car thieves. Some guys were strictly burglars. Some guys were strictly stick-up men. These were friends of mine. That's what they did. These were their fields of endeavor.

I've robbed people. I've broken into places. I've stolen cars. But none of them were ever my exclusive field of endeavor. I was never strictly a car thief. Never strictly a stick-up man. Never strictly a breaking-and-entering guy. I did a little bit of it all.

If I had a gun and an opportunity presented itself, I took advantage of it: "Let's rob that dude."

We robbed guys. We stuck people up. We strong-armed people. It was what it was. Some guys would say, "We're going to break into this store. You want to come?" I would ask a few questions about the lick, and then say, "Yeah, I'm in," or "Nah, I'm not."

One time, we came across a guy we knew, and he had gloves and sledgehammers. We said, "What's up?" He said, "I'm going through the wall of this business." He asked us if we wanted in on the caper. We passed. I wasn't trying to sledgehammer through a brick wall just to "hit a lick."

I tried not to do dumb licks. That would have landed me in the penitentiary.

A lot of times we robbed criminals—guys who were selling dope or stolen goods. They couldn't call the police and report the robbery. We had to watch our backs, though, and make sure we didn't get caught with our guard down and let them retaliate.

One time years later, after more than a decade of pastoring at my church, I was in a restaurant with my wife, and a guy was standing across the room staring at me. Huffing and puffing and swollen up.

We made eye contact. As he walked over, I asked: "You alright? Do I know you?"

"Yeah, you know me. You know me."

He leaned over me. "You robbed me that time, of a couple pounds of weed. You and your boy Terry robbed me."

As he said that, I stood up out of my seat. "Man, you better get out from over top of me."

I had been out of the streets for years. But just because I was a pastor, I wasn't going to let some guy catch me with my guard down.

"You remember y'all robbed me?" he said.

I remembered him. My boy Terry and I had beat him nearly thirty years before. I said, "Yeah, I remember. But I'm not the same guy now that I was back then. The guy that robbed you died in a church on Eddy Road in 1982. He was the one that robbed you. He died. I'm not that guy anymore."

He replied, "I know you. I know what you do; I know you're a pastor. I know where your church is at." But he was still huffing and puffing.

I lost my temper. "Well if you knew me then, you know me now. You better back up," I said. "I'm not giving you the money. I'm sorry—what do you want me to say? I'm not giving you the money. You're not getting the weed back. What do you want to do? You want to go out in the parking lot and fight? What do you want to do?"

Then my wife got up in the guy's face, and I had to calm her down.

I told him, "You knew the codes of the street then; it was get or get got. One of the two. You rob or you get robbed. You beat or you get beat. It is what it is. You slip, you pay for it. Code of the streets." He understood. He calmed down. We chopped it up a little bit, talked about days gone by and people we knew. I then invited him to come to church sometime. That was it. We parted as friends.

Afterward, my wife and I had to ask the Lord to forgive us for our anger.

* * *

Growing up, I tried to be an educated thug—a crook who read books and newspapers and watched the news on television.

I almost never went to class. I was *at* school every day—outside, in the lunchroom, in the study halls—but never in class. At all. Once over Christmas vacation, I told myself that when January started, I was going to start going to class. I was going to try to turn it around. I went to homeroom the first day after break. The teacher looked at me and said, "Who are you?"

All the kids started laughing.

"My bad. Where am I?"

I never went back.

I never went to any of my high school classes except one: American history, because I liked it. And I read all of the black literature I could find. *Go Tell It on the Mountain* by James Baldwin. All of the autobiographies and biographies—I loved them. *Yes I Can* by Sammy Davis Jr. *Manchild in the Promised Land* by Claude Brown. *Cool Cos*, Bill Cosby's story. Dick Gregory's autobiography, *Nigger*, is probably one of the greatest books I've ever read in my life. *Up from Slavery* by Booker T. Washington. *The Autobiography of Malcolm X*. I loved Wilt Chamberlain. I read his book, *Wilt: Just Like Any Other 7-Foot Black Millionaire Who Lives Next Door.*

I would go to history class on Friday, because Friday was test day. I would take the test and get an A. One day, the teacher snapped at the class: "You all are in here every day, and this guy here only shows up once a week, and he gets an A!" I gained a measure of satisfaction from that.

* * *

I had a 9mm handgun when I was sixteen. My brother and I carried it to school a lot.

In fact, a lot of my friends carried guns to school. Pistols, sawed-off shotguns. That wasn't anything unusual. One guy I knew even shot at a teacher in the parking lot.

One day I was sitting in a friend's car in the school parking lot, and the vice squad drove past. They saw me sitting there and for some reason came over, pulled me out of the car, and found the gun on me. They impounded the car, too. My friend was pissed.

The detectives who arrested me said I fit the description of someone who had been involved in a robbery, so it gave them a reason to detain me. *Yeah, right,* I thought. It was a classic case of stop and frisk.

When I went to court, the judge told me to go to school, stay out of trouble, get good grades, and come back in June with my progress. I went back to school the next week and promptly got suspended.

On my way home from school after getting suspended, I passed by the Army recruiting station that I passed every day. Something inside me told me to stop in that day. That whim would change my life. I walked in there and took the test. The recruiter told me, "You scored so high that you can pick any field you want to pick." I joined the Army on the spot.

Later on that night, I said to my mother and father, "What do you think about me joining the Army?" I was sixteen years old.

"I don't know," my father said. "That might not be bad."

"Good, because I already did."

I had signed up on the delayed entry program in 1975 and left in May 1976, before I was supposed to reappear before the judge in June.

I had never been outside Cleveland before. The Army changed me as far as my level of maturity was concerned, but it didn't change my character. I was still the same guy.

* * *

When I tell people that I am a veteran, they say, "Thank you for your service." Sometimes I question whether I should be thanked or whether I should give thanks.

I was stationed at Fort Gordon in Augusta, Georgia. Basic training was easy for me, as was advanced instructional training. I just followed orders, and everything was smooth. I didn't have a problem with authority, because my father was a disciplinarian. I was used to being yelled at. My family is a family of yellers. We all have thick skin.

My first day of advanced instructional training, I ran into some guys that I knew from Cleveland. A guy named Ron from my neighborhood was in uniform too. We immediately hooked up to smoke some weed, which he had. We went to an off-limits area to smoke and got caught. I received an Article 15 (nonjudicial punishment) and was put on restriction and got extra duties.

Terry would send me weed in the mail, too. He would write on the envelope, "Pictures. Do not bend." There would be four or five joints in there. I might not have made it through basic training without him.

I was a 72E telecommunications center specialist with top-secret clearance. When it was time for permanent duty, I was sent overseas to Frankfurt, Germany. After a short time there, I was given the option of going to Greece or Turkey. I chose Greece, because in my mind I envisioned pyramids. Uhhh...that's Egypt, stupid. But I fell in love with the country immediately. It was absolutely beautiful. The people were fantastic...and color blind. I enjoyed my time there immensely.

In Greece I was temporarily housed at the Transit Airmen's Quarters (TAQ) at Hellenikon Air Base. It was like a hotel. I robbed it my first day there. I was down in the lobby, and the front-desk man had left to go to the bathroom or something.

I told my friend Mike, who had been sent to Greece with me from Georgia, "He's not in the lobby. Let's rob that cash drawer."

"How do you do it?"

"You just snatch it open."

We went over. "Look out," I said, pulling open the cash drawer. I grabbed about five hundred bucks and took off.

In 1976, right after the Vietnam War, I was sent to a permanent duty station in Greece. I was seventeen years old and had a "gravy" job—twenty-four hours on, forty-eight hours off. During off hours, I gravitated toward those of my kind. I gravitated to the Army criminal element. I found myself in a situation with a guy named Jay who was on his way back to the States.

"I want to introduce you to some people," he said. Soon I was in the Greek black market, buying American-made products at the PX (the Post Exchange, a military retail store) and selling them to black marketeers to sell to Greeks at a huge markup.

I was AWOL a lot.

Once my master sergeant lost his temper with me. "Dammit, Scott. What's the matter with you? You've got an easy job! Twenty-four hours on, forty-eight hours off. What the hell is the matter that you're AWOL all the time?"

"Let me tell you something, Sergeant. The twenty-four hours on isn't the problem. It's that forty-eight hours off that's killing me."

I was in uniform but still a criminal. I got court-martialed and stripped in rank, but I didn't care. The Army was paying me $296 per month. The black market was paying me more than $500 a day. I loved it. I told myself I was never going back to America again, but eventually it came time for me to be discharged, and I went back home.

* * *

Upon returning home, I also returned to the streets. A little older. A little wiser. A lot more mature, having experienced Army life and the discipline that came with it. After having seen different countries with different cultures, I was not the same guy. I recommend military service for any young man who does not want to go to college. It can change the course of a life.

I got job in a Ford plant. I got hiring preference because I was a veteran. Twelve hours per day, seven days per week, eighty-four hours per week. Twelve dollars an hour, with time and a half for overtime and double time on weekends. I was taking home $1,400 a week at nineteen years old.

I sold a lot of dope when I worked at Ford, right inside the plant. Eventually, there was a big layoff. But I didn't mind, because I still had the streets. It was the same problem I'd had in the Army. Work was fine, but I loved that street life. That was me. It was in my blood.

Still, those Bibles that I had read when I was a kid subtly affected me. I had certain standards. I wouldn't kill anybody. I've shot *at* people just to scare them, but I haven't shot anybody. Even though I was out there on those streets with some stone-cold killers, something always restrained me from crossing certain morality lines.

I just didn't know how that something would eventually change me.

* * *

I met a guy named KD through a mutual friend from the neighborhood. He sold a lot of drugs and hosted concerts and parties. He had bought a nightclub downtown called The Mad Hatter. It was there that I met Willie D, his brother, who would become a close friend and mentor to me. I was about nineteen years old. Willie D was thirty-two.

He had everything I wanted: the money, the drugs, the cars, the clothes, the women, and the nightclub. I wanted to be in his circle; I wanted to be in his world. He took me off the streets and into the upper echelon of the drug dealers' world in Cleveland in the late seventies. He was also a businessman, having owned several beverage stores in the inner city. I became his assistant, protégé, confidant, driver, son. Whatever he had, I had. Whatever he drove, I drove. Whatever he ate, I ate. He shared everything with me, because he trusted me. And I never betrayed that trust.

He taught me everything. He taught me entrepreneurship. He taught me how to put up drywall. He taught me how to do electrical. He taught me how to do plumbing. He would say, "You go in there with those drywall men and you watch them so we won't have to pay them. You go in there and you watch them, and you ask them questions so you can learn how to do it yourself."

The nightclub was a big success. It was Cleveland's black version of Studio 54. There were lines around the corner every night to get in. We were in that life, that entertainment world of the black R&B artists, and of the drug dealers, pimps, and prostitutes. That was my world, those were my associates, and there was nothing unusual about it. To me, pimps, prostitutes, criminals, thieves, robbers, and killers were ordinary people with ordinary lifestyles. I saw nothing wrong with what they did.

I didn't see daylight for a couple of years, because the club opened at night. In daytime, like vampires, we slept.

FOUR

My world was about to collide with a respectable girl who would change my life forever. Her name was Belinda.

We had decided to try a new format at the nightclub. On Wednesday nights, the club was converted to strictly jazz and entertained a different class of clientele than we usually attracted.

Belinda was a jazz backup singer for a number of nationally known jazz artists. My guy Willie D had spotted her at an event downtown and begged her to come to work for us. She wasn't the type to patronize the nightclub, but the jazz world was her world, so she gave us a chance, coming on board as a Wednesday-night hostess.

There I was, a criminal from the street, and she was a sophisticated, nice girl from the jazz world. She wouldn't even go down to the club on Friday or Saturday night, but she was there on Wednesdays.

I'll never forget the first time I saw her. In a picture in a magazine. She had done some modeling for a photo shoot. Some of the guys had the magazine and were looking at her picture.

"Who is that?" I said.

"She works downstairs."

"Works downstairs where?"

"Works downstairs here." We all broke for the steps, running downstairs like a pack of wolves after prey.

I got downstairs first. She was walking outside, and I followed her out. I came out with my suave, mac daddy vibe. "Hey, baby, what's your name? I was checking you out in here. My name is Scotty. Let me get your phone number." She looked at me like I had lost my mind.

"Who do you think I am?" she said. "I'm an old-fashioned girl. You don't just walk up to me, asking me for my phone number like I'm going to give it to you. Psh!"

She turned around and walked off. I stood there frozen in my tracks. After regaining my composure, I went back inside. All the guys were waiting for me to give them the progress report. "How did it go? Did you get her number?" I said, "What's my name? Yeah, I got it." I was lying, though. Talk about a blow to a guy's ego.

Belinda disliked me immediately. I would see her every Wednesday night and try to get her attention, but she wouldn't give me a second look. I just wasn't her type. I was loud and boisterous. Every guy in that club was after her, but she didn't give anybody any traction. Months later, I was still smarting from our first encounter.

I didn't know it at the time, but she was harboring a hidden hardship that was part of her attitude, her distance.

One winter night, her car wouldn't start. Willie D asked me to see if I could get it started for her. I knew about cars from my car thief days. I went out there and got it started for her.

Her gratitude was very mixed. She was like, "Thank you. I don't like you, but thank you." To this day she thinks that I rigged her car to not start so I could go out there and start it. I'm not saying whether I did or didn't. The Bible says, "The things revealed belong to man, but the secret things belong to God." I'm gonna leave whether I rigged her car or not between me and God.

The club owner, KD, liked her and knew that she didn't like me. He would say, "I need you to give Belinda a ride home." So I started taking her home. Slowly, the conversations warmed up. A relationship began to develop. We were becoming friends.

Because she was a good girl, I couldn't interact with her the way I was used to interacting. I was used to street girls, girls that were in that street life like I was. Boosters, prostitutes, drug users, dealers. It was very challenging at first, interacting with a lady who required that I be a gentleman. I started liking her more and more, and she began seeing things in me that I didn't even see in myself. I found out that I didn't have to put up a pretense with her. I didn't have to be hard or gangster or street. She wanted to know the real me.

The trouble was, I didn't know who the real me was. I knew the me that I showed everybody, and I wasn't the type to be introspective. With me, what you saw was what you got. But she felt that underneath the facade, somebody else was in there.

We began to have a platonic relationship, and we spent more and more time together. Other girls tried to talk her into dropping me: "You shouldn't fool around with Scotty, because he's just going through one of his things."

Belinda has never been one to allow others to make up her mind for her. "That's alright," she said, "because I'm just going through one of my things, too."

When I heard that, I thought, *Whoa...I like this girl.* She had that dog-gone spunk. I liked it. I liked her.

It got to the point where I started having to choose: her house or the cesspool of pushers and prostitutes that the club was on weekend nights. I started skipping the club on weekends and hanging around her house.

I stepped away from that club life to be with her and started going down there only occasionally. I was still selling dope, though.

Then I learned her sad secret. Her mother was dying of cancer. Belinda would go take care of her mother, and then she would come back and cry in my arms all night. Her mother died in January 1981.

So at only twenty-two years old, Belinda had to care for all the children her mother had left behind. Her baby brother was fifteen years old, and her sister was sixteen. Her sixteen-year old niece was living there also.

Her younger siblings begged her, "Belinda, please. Belinda, please move back home." So she moved back to her mother's house where she had grown up, and I went with her. She tried to retain some sense of normalcy for her younger brother, who had lost his mother.

* * *

By this time, in 1981, cocaine users had graduated to freebasing. The powder causes too much wear and tear on a person's sinuses. We had begun smoking it in cigarettes, but then freebasing came out.

The funny thing about cocaine is this: if there is any redeeming virtue to it, it is that it's a jealous master. All you want to do is smoke it. You no longer want weed, booze, or any other intoxicant. I was a cocaine man. The cocaine kind of came in and displaced everything else.

I was selling PCP, but I was smoking cocaine.

One of the guys in the entertainment industry had taught me how to cook cocaine, how to make rocks. It was an acquired skill. Not a lot of people knew how to do it back then, and I was in demand among some dealers to cook for them, as they would have a "base ball game," as it was called back then. It was a new wave, for the elite. We didn't snort anymore. That was for the lower class. We based ours. It set us apart. Made us feel special. It hadn't become the epidemic that ravaged the black community yet. Freebasing was a new thing back then. It was just getting around in the community, and it was very addictive, because it produced an unequaled high. That's why it's so powerful—because anyone who does it can't help but like it. That's why I don't condemn those who are trapped in its grip. I feel sorry for them and try to help them.

However, my life was about to change.

* * *

One Friday night in 1982, I was spraying PCP on weed out of a spray bottle—making a value-added product. Reefer laced with PCP. It was called "wet." I was freebasing cocaine, but I was mainly selling wet. In order to freebase, we had to make a "torch" out of a cotton ball soaked in 151 rum on the end of a coat hanger, to keep the pipe hot enough long enough to smoke it. It was around half past six in the evening. I was getting prepared to hit the streets with product and make some money that night. But I ran out of rum.

In those days, rum was sold in state-run liquor stores that closed at 6 p.m. The only option to get liquor after 6 p.m. in the inner city was to go to an after-hours joint. These places were called "green doors."

I said to Belinda, "Go around the corner to the green door and get me a bottle of 151 rum." She left the house to walk around the corner to the store. She was gone for a long, long time. Because she didn't come back, I couldn't go anywhere and sell anything.

I never went out in the streets that night. I was more worried about her than I was about making money from selling dope. I hoped nothing had happened to her, but my hope was in vain. Something had happened to her.

When she finally came back home, it was after midnight, and she was speaking in strange words. Nothing made sense. *She must be high*, I thought.

Finally, Belinda started to explain. "I was outside and on my way to the store. I ran into Bubble, and I went to church with him tonight. I'm saved. You've got to go. You've got to move. I'm not doing this anymore."

"What? What are you talking about?"

"I went to church tonight, and it was just wonderful. The preacher preached, and you should have been there. I gave my life to Jesus. Now I'm a Christian. You've got to move. We can't keep doing this. I'm not doing this anymore."

"What the hell is going on?" I said. "What are you talking about?" Church? What?

That night, she wouldn't let me in the bedroom. "What is going on here?" I said.

She said again, "I'm not doing it anymore. I'm not sleeping with you anymore. I'm not doing it anymore."

She knew I was selling drugs; that's how I lived. That's how I got my income. She had a job, and she knew what she was getting into with me, but she liked me. We had fallen in love with each other. Now she wouldn't let me in the bedroom.

What the heck is going on here? *Boy*, I thought, *this girl is tripping*. But it was alright. The house we were living in, her mother's house, was big. Seven bedrooms. I slept in another room.

The next day was Saturday, and she was reading the Bible. *What is she doing?* I wondered.

She went to church the next day, but I didn't go. She went back that same night, too.

I was getting irritated. "Girl, how much church are you going to? You went Sunday morning; you're back Sunday night?" Every time she'd come back, all she did was talk about Jesus. That's all she did.

She broke up all of our albums and threw them away. "I'm not listening to that type of music anymore," she said.

What was going on with this girl? Now, we had no music to listen to. Instead, she listened to gospel radio stations. She changed her style of dress; her skirts became longer. She didn't wear open-toed shoes. She wouldn't bare her shoulders.

She kept telling me, "You have to move; I can't live with you anymore." She would even circle places for rent advertised in the newspaper. "You need to find a place to go. You need to find an apartment."

This went on for about two months.

It came to a head one Friday night in 1982. I had bought a whole lot of cocaine and PCP, and I was going out to make money that night. All my money was invested in this product. I was going out in the streets to sell it.

As she was on her way to church, like she had begun to do every Friday night, she turned around and begged me, as she had before: "Why don't you go to church with me tonight?"

As usual, I said no.

"Come on, go to church with me tonight. Please go." A tear was rolling down her face. "I just want you to come to church with me tonight."

I wouldn't. "Girl, I'm not going to no damn church. What are you talking about? I told you, quit asking me this crap."

She was full-on crying. It touched me, because Belinda is not a crying person. So I gave in. "I'll tell you what, I'll just go this one time. After that, don't ask me anymore." That was the deal. She agreed.

So I went to church with her that night, pretty high.

I walked in, very judgmental. It was not an opulent cathedral. It was a church in the hood.

The people there were very friendly to me. Belinda had made some friends, and they were glad to see her bring me to church with her that night.

After the choir sang, the bishop began his sermon, and the message that he preached was, "Go back to Bethel." I'll never forget. He talked about Jacob, who was in distress at a certain time in his life. God appeared to Jacob and told him, "Go back to Bethel; go back to the place where you first met me."

At the end of the sermon, the bishop said, "Is there anyone here tonight that wants to know Jesus Christ as your Lord and personal savior? Young man, young lady, you're not here by accident tonight. God brought you here tonight. It's not a coincidence. You need to stand up and give your life to the Lord."

I was sitting in a pew with others, but after a while, it seemed like I was the only person in the room. The bishop was saying, "If you want to give your life to Jesus, you need to come down to this altar."

I'm not getting up. I'm not standing up, I kept telling myself.

"If you want to give your life to Jesus, stand up."

I was in some type of vortex or something. *Skip this*, I thought, *I'm not doing this stuff.* Then, somehow, I found myself standing up.

"You need to make your way down to this altar right now and give your life to the Lord."

I told myself, *I'm not walking down to no altar*...but I felt my feet moving. I walked down there to the front.

"Lift your hands and pray this prayer after me," the bishop said.

I lifted up my hands and prayed that prayer, repenting my sins and asking Jesus to come into my life and make me clean.

After the prayer, the bishop said, "We're going to take you downstairs and baptize you."

On my way downstairs, I recognized one of the deacons who was walking with me to perform the Baptism ceremony. It was a guy I had grown up with.

The last time I'd seen him was in a drug deal, seven or eight or maybe nine years before. I hadn't seen him out on the street in a long time. Usually when guys vanished from the block, it was because they had gone to prison. But now I knew where he had gone.

He looked at me and said, "Welcome home."

It touched me. They took me down and baptized me. I came out of that water a new person and went back upstairs.

The pastor said, "You're saved now! You're a Christian."

I was feeling pretty good, but I felt a burden. I blurted out, "I've got drugs at home."

The pastor seemed unbothered. Nonchalantly, he said: "No problem. Just go home and get rid of them. I'll see you on Sunday."

He made it sound so easy that it empowered me. Belinda was crying; she was very happy. We had gone to church with the brother, Bubble, who had originally taken her there, and he was happy. I was happy. Everybody was happy. I had gone into that church dirty, but I had come out clean. Gone in a sinner and left a saint. It was the best day of my life.

I went home, gathered up all my dope, and went into the bathroom. Then it hit me. "Wait a minute! I can't flush this stuff down the toilet. All my money is tied up in this."

Belinda said, "Flush it." She sounded firm.

"No," I said. "Here is what I'm going to do: I'm going to sell it." It was a couple of thousand dollars' worth of cocaine and PCP. It was all bagged up, ready for distribution. "I'm going to sell it, and after that, I'm not going to sell anymore."

"God said get rid of it," she said. "Get rid of it all." I thought about it one more time, then I took the plunge. I emptied all the bags into the toilet. Everything I had.

Then I flushed.

Belinda started crying—tears of joy. I was standing there, looking funny and feeling funny.

I was instantly delivered.

I never used drugs again, from March 1982 until now. I never used cocaine again. I never even was tempted to use it again. I never had the craving or the battle. I never drank another drop of liquor or smoked another cigarette. I went cold turkey on everything. I was saved. It was a miracle.

But I had spent all my money on the product that I flushed, and had to get a new source of income. Now what was I going to do?

* * *

You know what made it easy for me, though? Belinda. Her salvation. As soon as she got saved, she was instantly a strong Christian. She witnessed to everybody. She told all her friends—all she did was talk about the Lord; all she did was talk about Jesus.

I didn't know anything about that. I was totally church illiterate. I still had that working knowledge of the Bible from those Bibles that I'd read when I was little, but I had no church experience. The one time I had gone to church, I kept a nickel out of the offering from the dime I was supposed to put in. I didn't know anything about church etiquette or church behavior.

Yet I knew four things: I was saved, I didn't sell dope anymore, Belinda was happy, and I had to find a real job.

And I had to find a job while walking, because one night around that time, Belinda's brother sneaked my car out of the driveway when I was asleep and totaled it.

* * *

My father helped me get a job at a hotel downtown, driving a shuttle bus. I discovered that if you want to be a Christian, the easiest way is keep it simple.

I didn't go around any of my old associates anymore. I had a regimen and stuck to it. I went to church, work, and home. Work, home. Work, home. Work, church, home. Work, church, home. Work, church, grocery store, home. That was the pattern I set for myself to keep it as simple as possible.

I didn't go anywhere that I used to go. I didn't go to any of my old stomping grounds. I didn't go in any of those old haunts. My friends didn't know where I was. They didn't know whether I was in jail or dead. They didn't know what happened to me. I totally vanished and immersed myself in work, church, and home.

* * *

We had been going to church for a couple of weeks. We were still living together but abstaining from fornication. People in the church knew we were living together, but nobody judged us. They said, "If they're really saved, the Holy Ghost will take care of it. We're just glad they're here."

We went to see the pastor, Stanley Hauton.

"Bishop, we're living together," I said.

"Yes, I know. Do you love her?"

"Yes."

"Do you love him?" he asked Belinda.

"Yes," she said.

"Be in my office tomorrow at noon."

The next day, I was working downtown at the hotel. I went and picked Belinda up, we went to the church at noon, and the bishop married us in his office. We never had a formal ceremony. It was just me, Belinda, and the pastor.

We went to McDonald's afterward. Then I had to go back to work.

We've been together ever since.

* * *

The local Christian bookstore became a part of my life. Every Friday when I got paid, I would go to the Christian bookstore and buy myself a book. Belinda and I read the Bible, but I always had to have another book to read. I'd take a book with me to work and read between my runs as a shuttle bus driver. Reading became a regular part of my Christianity, and I studied the Bible as much as I could. What I didn't know then was where all of that reading would lead.

* * *

Belinda and I were a married Christian couple. It was like a breath of fresh air, a rebirth. I was not the person I used to be. She was no longer the person she used to be.

We moved across town and joined an interracial church that a neighbor had invited us to visit. Our pastor was Italian. The congregation was around half-black and half-white when we joined. After about five years, it became 95 percent black and 5 percent white, which was disconcerting to our white pastor.

One thing about Belinda and me: when we get into something, we get all the way in. We can't be on the periphery. We couldn't be satisfied with just going to church, sitting down, hearing a message from the pastor, and then going home. We wanted to be in as much as possible. We volunteered to do as much as we could. I was the church bus driver, and my wife worked in the Sunday school and in the children's church. She sang in the choir. We worked in the food bank, distributing food to those in need every Thursday. We made a lot of friends in the church. We became pretty close with our pastor as well.

Around that time, cable-access television came around. We became the producers for our church's television broadcast. I would drive and pick up the equipment, and Belinda would come and help me set it up. We'd use an analog editor to edit the footage.

My wife started publishing and distributing her own gospel tracts.

We didn't go to the movies. We didn't watch non-Christian television. We didn't listen to anything other than gospel music. We attended church, were very active in ministry, and grew in our knowledge of the Lord and our relationship with God.

After six years, we changed our membership to a predominantly black church. We needed to experience another facet of Christianity, the Black Church. We joined a nondenominational church and became very active once again. It was there that we were ordained into the ministry.

* * *

After consulting with our pastor, we started our own church with four people in 1994. But there were never just four people in attendance. More always came. Twenty people came to our very first Bible study. The next week, twenty-five came. Then thirty. We did Bible study in February 1994, and our first Sunday service was in March.

Our church grew rapidly. By the time it was six months old, 150 members were on the register. The Lord gave us vision and provision.

Our church received a lot of criticism because of our success. Many people in Cleveland, and many Christians in general, objected to the idea of a female pastor—but my wife had been tag-team preaching ever since we started teaching together at our former church.

My view is different. One of the roles of the church is to re-create a family environment, and I believe that a two-parent home is the healthiest home and a one-parent home is unbalanced. So a husband-and-wife team makes sense to me.

My wife is a great pastor. She knows the Bible cover to cover, and she's a heck of a preacher. In fact, I think she's a much better preacher than I am. She has a great stream of consciousness and train of thought. She's very articulate and thought-provoking. She touches hearts.

In spite of challenges and criticism, we continued on in our own way, and the church grew. It started in a rented room in a former synagogue. The building was beautiful, with a large dome that sheltered a two-story worship center. The dome sat atop an Art Deco rectangle that housed two restaurant-style kitchens (two were needed due to kosher dietary laws), several banquet halls, and many classrooms and offices. It is a historic landmark...the first orthodox synagogue in Cleveland Heights. Any entity could rent a room for any kind of gathering.

We started in a banquet hall. Soon even that big room was crowded, so we moved into the main hall. The facility needed updates and renovation, and we raised several hundred thousand dollars and renovated that space. Within a few years, we purchased the entire facility.

So we started there with four members and wound up owning the building. A lot of churches have a nomadic existence, moving every few years. Our church has never moved.

Vision and provision.

Our facility is 120,000 square feet and a revenue-generating facility. We bought a gospel radio station and moved it into the building. We opened a daycare facility, employing our members and others in the community, as we continue to do now.

Over the years, our church established itself as one of the leading churches in the greater Cleveland area. We've hosted a number of community events, including concerts, conferences, women's academies, and television programs. We've hosted youth meetings, offered a ministry for substance abuse rehab, and provided many more services to the Christian community and the community at large, as we continue to do to this day.

FIVE

No matter what the critics said, I think Donald Trump made a great impression upon the black pastors gathered in Trump Tower that day in 2015. Even if they were not going to vote for him, they were not going to advocate against him. I know that for a fact. And some contacted me, saying: "I was very impressed by him, and I am going to vote for him, but I'm not going to advocate for him. I can't let anybody know."

They were frank enough to tell me that much.

With my background and being the type of person I am, I believe you're either a man or you're not a man. My first pastor used to always tell us, "You either stand for something, or you'll fall for anything."

Some of these guys fall for anything. Yet some brave souls stood out. Bruce LeVell stayed strong in the face of opposition. Pastor Mark Burns did also. Those were the main ones who didn't back down, roll over, or play dead. They fought in private and in public for then-candidate Trump and never wavered. I commend those guys for that.

The pastors who were the bravest tended to come from the smaller, less notable churches. I believe that they, like me, saw something in Trump that we all hoped could be conveyed to the America public.

* * *

Gradually, a team of supporters gathered around Trump, a number of them black, and he welcomed them warmly. And Omarosa took a very public stand for Trump. Prior to our meeting at Trump Tower, I hadn't seen her out there for him.

Omarosa wrote in her 2018 book, *Unhinged: An Insider's Account of the Trump White House,* that she helped plan the meeting of pastors at Trump Tower. That's funny, because I planned it and met her for the first time at the meeting. However, I don't want to discount her communication with Michael Cohen. If she did have anything to do with it, it was through Cohen.

Katrina Pierson, who is black, was offered the role of Trump's press secretary, which I thought was tremendous. Here was a black woman as a potential press secretary for Donald Trump, who is supposed to be a racist. I thought that the media should have recognized that fact, but people seem to discount that. The media had their narrative about Trump being a racist, and they were sticking to it.

It became a pretty tight-knit fraternity. We became more than friends. We became family. As I became more a part of the Trump campaign's inner circle, I met a lot of people I didn't previously know.

I met Corey Lewandowski, the campaign manager at the time. He had a very outgoing personality and was friendly with me from the very beginning; he immediately welcomed me. I liked him, and he liked me. Michael Cohen did not like Corey Lewandowski. Cohen hated nearly everybody in the campaign, probably because he did not have an official position within the campaign, and was often excused from campaign strategy meetings. He called himself "Trump's pit bull," and to a large extent he was. He was the pit bull who would bite Trump's friends. A guard dog is supposed to protect against intruders and enemies, not bite friends and family.

When I first met Corey, we talked simply about how we could engage with the campaign and be of help to it. As the campaign manager, he could have locked me out or hindered my progress into the inner circle, but he engaged me. I found it refreshing that he welcomed me in.

Corey is a tough SOB, and he's got King Kong–size balls. I gravitate toward people like that. He is very strong, focused, and courageous. He's the kind of guy I'd want on my side if I ever went into battle. He became a very close friend of mine, and I now consider him a brother. I go to him when I need to talk about certain things regarding this Trump administration.

Corey's receptionist was Cassidy Dumbauld. Cassidy and I became friends, and she was very valuable to the Trump campaign. She is now an assistant to Jared Kushner and one of the top women in Trump's administration. Cassidy doesn't seek the limelight, and is very efficient and effective. She's brilliant, a very hard worker, very focused, and very determined. She's great for this country.

Hope Hicks was another Trump team member I met at the very beginning. She was great—a dedicated, tireless worker. And Trump's secretary at Trump Tower, Rhona Graff, was very gracious toward me.

Dan Scavino is the guy who writes President Trump's tweets. He started out as Trump's golf caddy and went on to replace the general manager at one of Trump's golf clubs. Trump is spontaneous like that. Scavino did a tremendous job at that club. As a result, he kept getting promoted within the Trump organization. Now he's a right-hand man, a very valuable member of the Trump orbit.

There are so many more in the Trump orbit I want to mention—people with whom I have become great friends. Lynne Patton stands out; she's a fellow African American who ignored the media narrative and was very effective for the campaign. A score of other receptionists, secretaries, gofers, assistants, and volunteers also worked very hard to make Trump's 2016 presidential campaign a success.

Did I experience any racism? Not in the least. Color was never a factor in any of our relationships—one more thing the media is dead wrong about.

* * *

Hillary Clinton had a well-oiled machine; we had a motley crew. Trump has such great instincts, though, that he took people—some of us with no political experience—to that type of level. He didn't mind employing us. I guess he figured that we could speak to any man and every man.

This Trump crew worked. Cassidy worked. Corey worked. Scavino worked. Hard. Very hard.

It was a twenty-four-hour activity for everybody. Donald Trump is probably the hardest-working person I've ever seen in my life. I don't know where he gets his energy from.

One person who was not a part of the campaign was Michael Cohen. He was employed by the Trump organization, not the presidential campaign. And that irritated him. Cohen disliked anyone he saw as a threat—and a threat was anybody he saw as being closer to Trump than he was.

If Cohen kissed up to Trump, it was because he wanted to, not because he had to. Contrary to the popular fake-news narrative, Trump does not surround himself with sycophants. This guy is a New Yorker. New Yorkers are probably some of the frankest, bluntest people around. Trump would rather be told an unpleasant truth than a pleasant falsehood. He wants to know upfront when things are going bad so he can deal with them. That's the kind of guy he is.

* * *

Trump once said to me, "I talked to Puffy."

Puff Daddy, Sean Combs, was a friend of his from way back. Actually, the black New York entertainment community was very friendly with Trump.

"Puffy told me," Trump said, "that I don't sound right saying 'African American.'"

I replied, "You know you can't say 'black' anymore."

Trump asked, "Why not? You can say 'white' and I can't say 'black'?"

I said, "That's the way it is now. You can't say 'black' anymore."

He said, "Okay," and we both laughed.

Trump was born in 1946. The black community went through a number of name changes between that time and now. At first, we were called colored people. Then we were called Negroes. Then James Brown came out with that great anthem, "Say it loud, I'm black and I'm proud." So we went from being Negroes to being black. Around the late 1970s, we stopped being black and we began to be called Afro-Americans, then people of color, then ultimately "African Americans."

Trump and I were able to laugh about it. "You've got to say 'African American' now," I told him.

He shook his head. The very next day he had a rally. In that rally, he looked over and said, "There's my African American right there," and everybody got upset.

I thought it was funny, to tell the truth. I called him and said, "You weren't supposed to say it like that."

The use of the word "my," as in "my African American," was used by critics and the left-wing media to condemn his statement. They said "my" implied ownership, which sounds ridiculous. It was a term of endearment for him that meant "my friend."

When he sees me, he says, "My pastor."

When he'd see Hope Hicks, he would say, "My Hope."

When he'd see Corey, he would say, "My Corey."

When he'd see Kelly Anne Conway, he would say, "My Kelly."

That's how he is; that's what he says to this day. I've heard him say it a thousand times. He's not implying ownership or any stupid thing like that.

He and I are not uncomfortable in the least with each other when it comes to matters of race or conversation about race. I personally don't mind the use of the word "black." That's what I use, because I'm a child of the 1960s. "Say it loud, I'm black and I'm proud," said James Brown. Stokely Carmichael said that "black is beautiful."

Black. White. It's no big deal. "Black" is not an offensive term. I don't have a problem with a white person using it. There can be an intent behind either word, like when somebody says, "You black so and so," or "You white so and so."

But you can empower with words, as we learned from Dick Gregory. The title of his autobiography is *Nigger*. In the book dedication to his mother, Lucille Gregory, he wrote: "Mama, from now on, whenever you hear the word 'nigger,' you'll know they're talking about my book."

Right there, he took the sting out of the word. He disempowered the word through his use of it. Words gain or lose strength through their usage and application. It's up to the individual whether or not to give words strength.

Gregory set out to destroy the power of that word. People today need to follow his example.

* * *

You know who defended me the most from the anti-Trump goons on social media? The guys I grew up with in the street. They would say, "Hey, watch your back out there. You can't trust these people," or "Hey, you're down with Trump. I ain't rolling with Trump, but I'm rolling with you. I don't know about Trump, but I know you," or "You need somebody to get your back, we got you."

These guys are supposed to be the sinners—the criminals. But the ones I grew up with know who I am, what I do, and they respect it. They're the ones who tell me, "Hey, one of these days, when I get right, I'll be over there [in church]."

Some of these are guys have done twenty or more years in the penitentiary. Some are still out there on drugs. But they stood by me. They were glad to have a friend who was a friend to a billionaire presidential candidate. They would email me, call me. They were proud of me. They would laugh and say, "Hey, man, tell Trump to break me off some dough." They would ask me, "Is Trump cool?" Some would ask, "Is he a racist?" And they would take my word when I'd tell them no.

Even people like Jesse Jackson Sr., who has been a friend of mine for several years, told me, "Listen. You're over there on that side. I can't go over there. I don't back Trump, but that's your choice. That's your prerogative. But just in case he wins, we need one of our people in that camp, in that inner circle."

I respected him for that.

Don King was another. He's been good friends with Trump for decades. King owns a historic black newspaper in Cleveland, *Call & Post*. After that meeting at Trump Tower with the preachers, the other newspapers in Cleveland were all attacking me. King told the people at his newspaper, "You better not put your mouth on him. He's one of ours. He's a Cleveland native; he's a good guy. I don't want you to print one negative thing about him."

I applaud guys like that.

* * *

As I said, Michael Cohen didn't like Corey. When Dave Bossie and Steve Bannon came aboard, he didn't like them either. He told me, "Those are some bad dudes. Don't have anything to do with those guys." It was his insecurity talking, not an objective view of Dave and Steve. He was afraid that the new guys would take his place at Trump's side.

How do I know this? Because Cohen repeatedly peppered me with requests to boost his stature with Trump. "Did you talk to the boss?" "Have you spoken to the boss?" "Did you ask him about me?" "Did you tell him about me?" "Speak to the boss about me."

In any case, I wasn't going to let him make up my mind for me. Steve and I became good friends. I first met Dave when he and I traveled to Detroit and went to Bishop Wayne T. Jackson's church. We rode together with Trump in the car. I liked Dave from the very beginning, and he and I are very close friends to this day.

* * *

For my first national television appearance, the topic was Donald Trump's criticism of then-presidential-candidate Ben Carson. I hadn't heard the comments they were referencing; I was hearing them for the first time live on the air.

On the split-screen panel with three other guests, I really didn't have time to process any thoughts about the comments Trump had made. Luckily, I was the last to talk. While I was sitting there wondering what the heck to say, one of the guests stated that Trump's criticism of Carson was not very presidential.

That's it, I thought. *I've got it now.*

"Presidential?" I said. "What's presidential? If you look up 'presidential' in the dictionary, what's the definition? When Bill Clinton played the saxophone on *The Arsenio Hall Show*, was that presidential? When Barack Obama danced on Ellen DeGeneres's show, was that presidential? Explain to me exactly what presidential is."

They were all quiet. I laughed out loud.

I never answered the question about Ben Carson and what Trump had said about him. I learned the art of deflection on the fly. All of a sudden, I was on TV with political pundits, against seasoned political observers, and had to debate these people. I was in over my head but didn't want anybody to know it. I learned early on that if I can't win a debate, turn it into an argument. I had a lot of fun doing that. I'm not going to lose an argument.

I was out there all the time winging it. The campaign rarely gave me any talking points, because Trump said: "You don't have to give him any talking points. Just let him go. He'll be alright."

Some would say, "You're a pastor. How can you talk like that?"

My reply was, "If I'm a pastor, respect that then. Talk to me like you respect me the way you should respect a pastor. You're not going to disrespect me or call my profession into question just because I support Donald Trump! Do you want the pastor, or do you want the street guy? Because if you want the street guy, you're going to get the street guy."

I remember one since-fired CNN contributor saying that Trump surrounded himself with some "mediocre Negroes." I wasn't going to take that. I responded by calling him a "little colored boy." He didn't like that.

I once told some black CNN contributors live on the air, "The things you read about in the history books, I lived through it. The civil rights movement that you read about, I lived through it. I lived through them rioting in the streets. My very first interaction with police was getting beat up by the cops. You're talking about the cops killing people—killing black people. I've got friends that got killed by police.

"Don't think because I support Trump that I'm detached from black issues. I'm very well aware of them from a personal standpoint. You've never been beat up by the cops. I have. You've never been fearful for your life with police. I have. You've never had friends that were murdered by cops. I have. Don't think that because I'm with Trump, I'm not in touch with the pulse of the black community."

Mike Tyson once said to some reporters, "You wouldn't last five minutes in my world." That's how I felt about those black CNN contributors.

I'd tell those guys, "If you be civil with me, I'll be civil back." I'm very aware when somebody tries to disrespect me or mock me. I don't take that crap.

I had a lot of heated exchanges with the media, like CNN. To me, the black people on CNN were as soft as Charmin. Cream puffs. They would try to "man up" a little when the camera was on, but when the camera would go off, they would try to shake my hand in private. I could tell that when the camera was on, they felt they had an advantage over me because of their political experience. They were lawyers, educators, pundits. But to me, they were a bunch of chumps.

I said to one, "You must have been a sorry lawyer, because I'm out-arguing you and I'm not a lawyer."

On CNN, I did Erin Burnett's show a lot. I did Anderson Cooper's show a lot too. I did Don Lemon but not as much. Burnett and Cooper are white, and they would always pit me against blacks. They were playing identity politics, playing the race card. They were doing what people say the slave owners did when they would get the slaves to fight each other for the master's amusement.

Once I asked, "Why are you always coming to get me to fight against other blacks? Why do you always have black people on, fighting against each other?"

Our people are more emotional, more combative by nature, which I like in an opponent. Angela Rye has a fiery personality. Tara Setmayer has a fiery personality. Bakari Sellers is a little softer-spoken, but he's very intelligent and very articulate. Van Jones is a good guy whom I consider a friend. He's on the opposite side of the political spectrum and is a very capable debater. Even though all of these people are refined and somewhat sophisticated, they haven't lost that emotion and combativeness.

I respect Angela Rye and Tara Setmayer. They don't really know me. All they know is the argumentative Trump supporter they fight with on television. If they knew me, I believe they would like me. I have strong opinions. I respect their opinions, and they should respect mine. I don't dislike them because they're on the left, but some of them dislike me because I'm on the right.

In my mind, we can argue passionately, vociferously, emotionally, but impersonally. We can go toe-to-toe, but when the camera goes off, we're still humans. Whether we're on the right or the left, whether I'm conservative and they're liberal, our blackness still connects us. We still have a shared history, a shared pain.

I don't believe that they think of me like that, but I think of them like that.

Sometimes I would mess with them for no other reason than I like to joke around a lot. In 2018 I tweeted, "Tyler Perry just announced that he wants Angela Rye to star in 'Diary of a Mad Black Woman 2.'"

I put that out there, and she was mad as a hornet's nest. She responded by calling me a "coon, a Tom." She has a law degree and should have had a more intelligent and articulate response than that. I think I woke the "hood" up in her. I actually got a good laugh out of my comment and her response. If I weren't a pastor, I would hit back a lot harder than I do.

The Democratic Party is supposed to be the party of tolerance. The party of acceptance. "You can't say this word; you can't be biased. You can't body-shame. You can't say derogatory terms about people. You'd better tolerate the gay community. You'd better give women their deference. You have to give any people of any race, creed, or color their deference." But you can call me a coon? That's alright? The only people in America that it's okay for liberals to be intolerant of are Trump supporters. You could kill a Trump supporter, and the liberals would think it was justifiable homicide.

Bull Connor was a Democrat. George Wallace was a Democrat. The party of racism in the civil rights struggle was the Democratic Party. Most blacks belong to or support that party, and they have the nerve to call me a coon.

SIX

The day before the election, Monday, November 7, 2016, just after Trump had finished his whirlwind tour, I went to Trump Tower. Everybody was coming "home" to Trump Tower the day before the election. Everybody in the war room was as busy as bees in a hive.

Hillary had four hundred employees over in her building. As I mentioned, she had a well-oiled machine and we had a motley crew. Everybody on our team multitasked.

I took a friend of mine up to the twenty-sixth floor of Trump Tower, the executive floor. Trump was back in his office for the first time in a long time. He looked around, and I said, "What do you see?"

He didn't know what I was talking about. "What? I see people working."

"If you let the media tell it, it's supposed to be Aryan Nations up here. You're supposed to have everybody sitting around in white hoods and robes. What do you see?"

It was a melting pot: Hispanics, whites, blacks, Asians. Whites were actually the minority. I often wondered why Trump never mentioned this. Then I realized he wasn't going to use his people as props. He had more respect for them than that.

Or maybe he just didn't think about race. A team of people from all backgrounds was just normal to him.

* * *

One of my favorite moments from the campaign was in Detroit, on that trip to visit Bishop Wayne T. Jackson's church that I mentioned. After the church visit, we were going to visit the house that Ben Carson had grown up in.

Trump said, "Come ride in the motorcade with me." Pastor James Davis rode with us, too. As we were riding through the streets of Detroit, we saw a street vendor who had cut a barrel in half and was selling barbecue on the sidewalk. You could smell it in the car.

"Is it any good?" Trump wondered.

"Heck, yeah. That's some of the best barbecue you're ever going to get," we said. Trump asked, "Do you think we should stop and get some?"

We said, "We can't stop. We've got a motorcade. The streets are blocked off. We've got motorcycle cops thirty deep down the street."

"Yeah, you're right," Trump said. "That's alright. I've got food coming to the plane."

After we left Ben Carson's house, we headed to Trump's plane, Trump Force One. I hadn't been on it yet, but I'd heard about how nice it was and was excited. Plus, we were very hungry.

I thought, *I wonder what we're going to eat. I wonder if they're flying the caviar in from Alaska. I wonder if the salmon has been flown in fresh from Norway. What are we having?*

Filet mignon, pheasant under glass, lobster tails? I mean, this man's a billionaire. He has exquisite taste when it comes to luxury, and I figured food shouldn't be an exception. He's owned world-class restaurants with world-class chefs and world-class food.

As we were sitting on the plane, Trump came over and said, "The food is here."

He was carrying the food to serve us: a platter full of Big Macs, Quarter Pounders with cheese, fries, McNuggets, all the cuisine that McDonald's has to offer. He was genuinely excited. I actually was not surprised.

That was part of his appeal to me and millions of others: the ability to "walk with kings and keep the common touch."

Trump is a McDonald's guy.

You've gotta love it!

Trump can be very amusing when it comes to food even when he's not on his plane. A couple of years later, on the night of the 2018 midterm elections, I went to the White House. It was a Who's Who of important people in America there, by invitation only from the president.

There were two buffets, one on each side of the room. On one side was the White House buffet: carved roast beef, carved turkey, and other elegant food. On the other side were pizzas, hot dogs, hamburgers, and french fries. Guess which side the president was on? He stopped over at the elegant side and greeted everyone there, but he ate on the pizza and hamburger side. One thing that man loves is a good hamburger. I like that about him.

As I said, Trump has the common touch. Here's another example. Soon after he was elected president but before he was inaugurated, I brought NFL legend Jim Brown to Trump Tower with me. We had a very good meeting downstairs and were afterward invited up to Trump's office on the twenty-sixth floor.

Trump was sitting at his desk, and three or four guys were standing in front of it. One of them was Bill Gates. But Trump didn't act like, "I've got Bill Gates here; you guys stay away. The election is over, so you black guys get out of here." No, that never happened. He greeted me like an old friend, introduced me around the room, and then focused his attention on Jim Brown. He was actually more excited about Jim being there than about Bill Gates.

* * *

As far as I know, I didn't have an antagonistic relationship with anyone in the Trump orbit. Paul Manafort was brought onto the campaign during the spring of 2016, and Corey was fired soon after. I didn't interact with Paul much, but we respected each other. His wife was very nice and friendly. We spent a little time together at the 2016 Republican National Convention in Cleveland.

When Rick Dearborn invited me to speak at the RNC, I was humbled and considered it a privilege. I would be making history that night; I don't know of any black preachers from Cleveland who have ever spoken at the RNC. I would be speaking on the main stage, during prime time. I already knew Rick Dearborn and Paul Manafort had signed off on it, and, of course, Trump had to approve it.

Michael Cohen was being his usual self about it. When I told him that I had been asked to speak at the RNC, he said, "Oh yeah, I did that. I told them to do it."

I don't know if he did or didn't.

I was contacted by the RNC's speechwriter. The Republican Party didn't want the speakers to be unprepared.

I said, "Look, I talk for a living. I'm used to speaking in front of a crowd; this is what I do. I write a speech every Sunday."

Everybody else had speechwriters working with them, but they let me write my own speech. I had to attend the rehearsal, however; and I aced it on the first try. My entire focus was on keeping my speech within the allotted minutes, because we preachers can get long-winded sometimes.

The night of the RNC, I was in the back with some of the other scheduled speakers, and I literally had to pray for them because they were nervous. I don't blame them. More than twenty thousand people were in the arena.

Laura Ingraham went on before me. They gave each of us eight minutes; Laura took sixteen.

A person came to the back and said, "Laura has gone too long, and we're going to be running over. Is it possible for you guys to cut your speech?"

"No!" I said. "I'm not cutting my speech. You better go out there and tell her to get off, or else I'll go out there and tap her on her shoulder. But I'm not cutting my speech."

They had the applause meter and said that up until that point, I got the most applause out of anybody. That night on CNN, Don Lemon complimented me.

"It seemed like we were at a church service. Were you nervous?" he asked me.

"No, I wasn't nervous; this is what I do."

When I finished my speech, the guy behind me said, "Now I've got to follow you, but I'm going to go out there and do my best."

We were all rooting for one another. As each person finished, we would all pat him or her on the back. Everyone did a great job—even Laura, who went overtime.

Afterward, we were in Trump's skybox, and Michael Cohen was there. He was a sad sack that night, raining on my parade. Everybody else was congratulating me and saluting me, saying: "You did a great job."

But I couldn't bask in my eight minutes of fame and of everybody patting me on the back, because Cohen was in my ear, whining and crying about how they didn't let him speak.

Trump came in and said to me, "There's my guy right there. Great job."

Cohen said to me, "Look, the boss knows I'm mad at him. I'm not going to speak to him."

Trump didn't pay any attention to this guy. Walked right past him. Cohen bellyached all night long. I had my wife with me, but I couldn't enjoy the moment.

The RNC had several events all day long and had different media tables, booths, and cameras set up. I would be doing media all day, and Sean Hannity had me on his show every night. Roland Martin, who had criticized me heavily on social media, was there. When I saw him, I said, "Roland Martin, my frenemy."

I put my fist up and waved it at him. Diamond and Silk were on his program, and they ripped him a new one and walked off. I loved it. Then

I wound up going on his show, and he and I argued about "the black people's plan" that he felt the president should have. I didn't understand how a person who had accused another person of being a racist would want the accused to have a plan for their race.

Don King came in; he was upset because Reince Priebus wouldn't let him speak at the RNC. Trump loves Don King, who'd already been his buddy for years, and wanted him to speak; but Priebus knew that if Don got up there and got that mic, you could kiss that eight minutes goodbye. He would have taken over the entire RNC.

Don was mad as a hornet's nest. He saw me and said, "I'm sticking with you." He's a Clevelander; I'm a Clevelander. As we were walking through, the reporters swarmed him, and he bashed Reince Priebus, calling him "Reese Primbus": "Reese Primbus won't let me speak."

I don't know who the poor guy was who was onstage at that time, but we walked into the main arena, and when we walked down those steps, Don came in loudly and sucked all the air out of the room. Everybody turned around: "There's Don King!"

All the attention went from the guy onstage to Don. All the microphones were in his face. It got to the point that security was needed and Don got his own mic—and he held court for over an hour. That was one of the funniest moments of the RNC.

Andy Dean was a guy I came to know during the campaign. He was an outspoken surrogate for the president, and during the RNC, I ran into him there. I had Pastor James Davis with me, and my closest assistant, who is both a brother and a son to me, Andrew Mixon. There was a time during the convention when only the delegates were allowed down on the floor. That day was picture day for the delegates who would be entered into the Library of Congress or entered into the Smithsonian. Andy Dean, James Davis, and I wanted to get on that picture, even though we weren't delegates. After we were refused admittance to the main floor, we all split up and went our separate ways. I didn't know Andy was going to sneak in, I didn't know James was going to sneak in, and they didn't know I was sneaking in. We each snuck in through different sections and were surprised to run into each other on the main floor. It was hilarious. We're in the delegate picture together, us four, standing with our hands reached out to the camera. If you go look at that picture, you'll be able to look out into the crowd and you'll see four non-delegates. Andrew Mixon, James Davis, Andy Dean, and me, all down on that floor together during the RNC. That was a great time.

I met many wonderful people during the RNC with whom I'm still friends, such as actor Robert Davi. I met Gayle King, who was very nice. Omarosa was there, and she introduced me to a lot of people. I got a lot of phone numbers, shook a lot of hands, took a lot of pictures.

* * *

One day, Trump had opposition in the GOP primary, and the next day, the opposition was gone. Those are the types of battles found in the Bible. One day the enemy is there, and the next day, God would step in and the enemy is defeated.

All Trump's opponents dropped out of the race at the same time.

I talked to him right after that. Trump said, "Can you believe this?"

"No," I replied. A couple of days ago you were going almost head-to-head with Ted Cruz and John Kasich, and now you're in the field all by yourself."

The dust settled, the smoke cleared, and Donald Trump was the last man standing. He was the presumptive nominee of the Republican Party for president. It was amazing.

* * *

Hillary took off during the summer of the campaign, because traditionally, politicians take off during that time. Trump never took off; he worked. Obama even came out and said that he outworked Hillary. Trump worked his butt off, and it was contagious.

I was given unlimited access in the campaign, and I made friends with a lot of people. Once, after Paul Manafort got fired, I was with

Trump on the campaign trail in Cleveland. He was scheduled to speak at a charter school and then at a fundraiser in Tony George's restaurant. Tony is a prominent businessman in Cleveland.

Trump told me, "Come on, go to the fundraiser with me. I'll put you in a room with a bunch of millionaires."

We went. The front part of the room that we were in was curtained off, and we were in the back. Trump went out to the front and gave his signature speech:

"We're going to build the wall, and Mexico is going to pay for it. We're going to do this...and make America great again."

When he finished, he sat with my friend Pastor James Davis and me in the back. We ate hamburgers and french fries. At one point, Trump actually served us. He said, "Those hamburgers are good; let me get you another one."

* * *

Trump was dead serious about winning. At that fundraiser, I found out how serious he really was. Paul Manafort had been fired by that point, and Kellyanne Conway had been hired as the new campaign manager. I was very impressed by her. Kellyanne is one of those folks I call "the undefeated." I've never seen her lose a debate or allow the media to get the best of her. I've never seen her confused or unsure or even hesitant when arguing a point or articulating her position. I've said that to her on many occasions: "You're still undefeated. Fifty to zero, with fifty knockouts."

At the fundraiser, I turned to Trump and said: "You're rewriting the rules of the game."

"What do you mean?"

"With most candidates, campaign managers are 'ride or die.' They get the same campaign manager and it's sink or swim. The campaign manager is with the candidate from beginning to end. You fired Corey, and then you fired Manafort; you're on your third campaign manager."

Trump didn't seem to think that firing campaign managers was that big a deal.

I said, "Kellyanne Conway seems to be good; she seems like she'll do a good job."

Trump looked at me and said something I'll never forget: "No slight to Kellyanne, but I will fire her the night before the election if that's what it takes for me to win."

Many people were saying that he didn't really want to win, that he was running for publicity; I knew better. Trump is a builder and a developer; he's a project oriented, goal-oriented guy.

Developers tend to categorize people according to their areas of expertise and the need of the moment, and interact with them accordingly. They look at the overall project and then engage with whoever is vital in whatever particular phase they are working on. They deal with the electricians, the plumbers, the drywall guys, the mud and tape guys, the carpet layers, the painters...whoever is necessary at the time.

That's how Trump the builder knew how to beat the competition—by being innovative and by rewriting the rules of engagement. He was serious from the start.

* * *

The media divulged a recording from 2005 of private citizen Donald Trump having a private conversation that he did not know was being recorded, with Billy Bush, who was at that time a correspondent on the TV show *Access Hollywood*.

I think Trump gave the perfect response to that: "It was locker room talk." A lot of men brag about their accomplishments and conquests, and exaggerate about their interactions with women.

Ninety-five percent of what is said you have to take with a grain of salt.

The media and his Democratic opponents tried to nail him to the wall for speaking hypothetically. Trump basically said that when you're famous, a lot of female fans will allow you to get away with almost anything.

I'm not condoning it, but it was a private conversation between private citizens. He didn't know he was being taped. His opponents probably released it a little bit too early, though. That was a tactical blunder.

Trump didn't allow people to bait him into keeping that conversation going. He said what he said, he issued his apology, and he moved on with it.

After that, they started trotting out women who said he had groped them. At a rally in Cleveland, I said to him, "You catching it at home? All of these people coming out and saying you groped them?"

He just gave me that look that every husband knows and shook his head.

* * *

The day before the election, we were at Trump Tower, and I was a bit nervous about how we were looking. Trump seemed relaxed. If he was nervous, he sure did a great job concealing it.

Everybody was working. I was floating around, socializing. Brad Parscale, Trump's data guy at the time (as of this writing, he's now the campaign manager for President Trump's 2020 reelection campaign), was there with a Nerf football. Brad is about six foot eight. We were eating pizza and throwing the Nerf football around.

I said, "Brad, come on, what's the skinny? Tell me something."

He said, "We're doing better today than we were doing yesterday. I got the early data in. We've got this."

I said, "What do you mean?"

He went over to his laptop and opened it. He said, "Do you see here, here, here, and here? I've got data from early voting. We're overperforming here, here, here, and here. We're going to win this election."

Meanwhile, CNN and MSNBC were saying that all the polls indicated Hillary would win by a landslide.

* * *

That night, Sean Hannity's show came on. Hannity preached that night. That's what we say in the Black Church world, when somebody's done a great job—we say, "man, he preached." Sean Hannity's pre-election night opening monologue was superb. He poured out his guts. By the time he finished, I was standing on my feet in front of the television with my hand in the air like I was in church.

He said, "America, you're going to own this if you don't vote for Donald Trump."

He spoke from his soul. He was very passionate. If he didn't touch anybody else in America, he touched me that night.

* * *

On Election Day, I walked into the lobby of Trump Tower, cautiously optimistic. In fact, everybody was cautiously optimistic. I went up on the twenty-fifth floor, and Keith Schiller, the president's head of security for decades, said, "The boss is here. Do you want to see him?"

I said, "Yes." I went into then-candidate Trump's executive office, and he was in great spirits. He was back at his desk for the first time in months, and you could tell that he was glad to be back in his office. He had a very messy desk, which was good. There were blueprints, drawings, plans, reports, a lot of checks for him to sign, and more. I like messy desks. My desk is always messy. A messy desk is the sign of a busy man.

Melania walked in.

I asked her, "How are you? How is Barron? How is he able to put up with all of the controversy?"

She said, "I try to protect him from the negativity. Supervise what he's allowed to watch and what he's not allowed to watch." Then she added, "He's heavy into sports. He plays soccer a lot. I try to keep him in a safe space, a safe environment."

I commend her for that. His parents wanted him to grow up with as normal of a childhood as was possible for a billionaire's son to have.

I asked the president, "Today is the big day. Man, here we are—this is it. What do you think?"

He said, "Hey, we'll see."

Donald Trump put me at ease on Election Day. He's got a million-dollar smile. He appeared so relaxed, it caused me to relax.

I went back down into the war room looking for Brad Parscale. He takes me into his office, and he's got four huge monitors all linked to each other. He's showing me all these stats and graphs and charts, and breakdowns by state and everything. Eric Trump came in, and we all scrutinized the charts and graphs on Brad's computer.

Afterwards, I went back to the hotel to get ready to go over to the campaign's central headquarters.

We arrived at election night party. Pastor James Davis and his wife, Michelle; my wife, Belinda; Youngstown businessman J. J. Cafaro and his lovely wife; and Steven Strang, the publisher of *Charisma* magazine, were all part of my entourage. My friends Francesca Nestande and Alyssa from the *Hannity* show, Sarah Huckabee Sanders, Gina Louden, Judge Jeanine, Sebastian Gorka, Omarosa, Bruce LeVell, and Mark Burns were also there.

Everybody in the Trump orbit—all the campaign workers and the supporters—was at that hotel that night to watch the election returns. We took selfies and had a wonderful time. I was able to meet Trump's brother, Robert Trump, that night. He's a great, great guy. The president's sister was there as well, and they were very proud of their brother.

As each state's returns came in, we would put the responsibility of carrying that state on whoever we knew who was from that state. Bruce LeVell, who is from Atlanta, was there with us, and Georgia came up. We were like, "Okay, Bruce, you've got to bring Georgia home. If we don't win Georgia, it's on you, buddy." Then we won Georgia, and Bruce was off the hook.

It came time for Ohio, and everybody was looking at me: "Okay, it's Ohio; it's on you." Ohio went for Trump. I was off the hook.

We let people from some states off the hook in advance. Gina Loudon is from California, and we all said, "Gina, we know we're not getting California, so we're not going to hold that against you."

As the early returns started coming in, it was Trump, Trump, Trump, Trump. We had gotten used to winning during the primary. Winning had become normal. This was simply a continuation of the success that we had been enjoying from the outset of the campaign. Nobody was surprised.

As Trump won one state after another, everyone would cheer. Every now and then, Hillary would win one, and we would boo.

The election was all but in the bag, and everyone was euphoric. The final announcement was only a formality.

When Trump won the election, we were still at the hotel. Staffers came and got me, saying: "Stand right here. When the president comes out, we want you to stand onstage with him."

I stood where they told me to for over an hour. Hillary was refusing to concede. John Podesta was on television saying, "Everybody can go home. We're not conceding yet."

I got tired of standing there. After more than an hour and a half, I left to go sit down on the floor. We'd been standing for hours. It was four o'clock in the morning when Hillary conceded.

The president walked toward the stage. A staffer called to me, "Okay, the president is going onstage. Come on, stand up with him."

I passed. Maybe I should have gone up there, but I didn't. It was his moment, not mine.

As I was out in the audience, I saw Brad standing onstage with Trump. Brad is so tall that he could see over everyone in the room. He scanned the audience, made eye contact with me, and mouthed, "I told you."

And he gave me the thumbs-up.

* * *

The first person I called after Hillary Clinton conceded the election was Corey Lewandowski.

"Corey, if it wasn't for you, we wouldn't be here. You had a big hand in this. You're like a starter in a relay race. You should be here. Because if it wasn't for you, this night would have never happened."

Corey is very courageous in public, but he's very humble in private.

He said, "We all did, we all played a part."

I said, "Well, I still wish you were here tonight."

He said, "Thanks, my friend."

The second person I called was one of my favorite people on earth, Sean Hannity. He was very friendly to me from the beginning. I love that guy. He is a very, very humble, very good guy—one of the best guys I know. Sean Hannity is my brother.

On the phone with Hannity, I told him he should've been there.

He said, "I'm at home watching it."

"Listen. You played a very large part in this victory."

"We all did," he replied.

"I'm telling you, that speech last night moved me," I said. "I wish you were here."

In 2017, Sean invited me to his Christmas party at an Irish tavern in New York. Ainsley Earhardt was there, as well as Francesca and Alyssa and a number of others who were a part of his team. And you know what we did at that Christmas party? Talked about the Bible all night long. It wasn't raucous; it wasn't wild. Sean Hannity is a very spiritual guy. Ainsley is a born-again Christian.

It was a Christmas party where all we did was talk about the Bible all night long. We talked about the Bible. All night long. Sean wouldn't want me to tell this, but I'm telling it anyway. This was during the time when people were boycotting my church, and he said to me, "How's the church doing?"

"We're doing alright, in spite of..." I said.

"You need anything?"

"No, I don't need anything."

"You sure you don't need anything?" Then he pulled his checkbook out of his pocket and wrote a check for a sizable donation right on the spot, made out to my church. That's the kind of guy he is. Reached into his pocket and wrote my church a check.

He said, "I know your church is suffering because of this. If you ever need anything, don't you hesitate to ask."

And he was firm: "Don't you tell anybody."

I appreciated the offer and the donation. One thing I can say about Sean Hannity: he has a heart for God. He studied religion when he was younger, and has a very good knowledge and understanding of the Bible. I think when his broadcast career is over, he will probably work in ministry, because that's where his heart is. I wouldn't be surprised to see him pastoring someday.

* * *

Against overwhelming odds, our candidate won the presidency of the United States. We won the battle. We were all amazed, but not surprised. We have war stories to tell, a shared history, a common pain, a bond, a shared struggle.

The very next day after the election, I was back at Trump Tower. Steve Bannon and I were about to get on the elevator, and Steve said, "Don't get on. Hold on, wait a minute."

We took the next elevator, just the two of us. As the door closed, we started slapping five with each other. "Can you believe this? We won!" Just two brothers on that elevator together, patting each other on the back and slapping five. We must have done it fifty times. It was like when a team scores a winning touchdown or field goal or home run. Then the elevator reached our floor, we straightened up, the door opened, and we walked out, totally normal. Nobody was the wiser. He and I shared that private moment after the victory, and it was very good.

* * *

I went back to Cleveland happy and relieved at the same time. After the dust settled and the smoke cleared, some people began to be curious as to what their role would be now that Trump was president. Not me. I felt like King David. The Bible speaks of David's being anointed by the Prophet Samuel: "After he pronounced to David that he would be king, David went back to tending sheep." Now I could go back to tending sheep and tending to my church.

The election was certified on November 10, 2016. I went back home and started receiving congratulatory phone calls from around the country, from a lot of different people, including preachers—even from those I knew were criticizing me and working against me behind my back. I'm not vindictive; I'm not like Omarosa was when she said she was going on a campaign to make everybody bend a knee. I feel like politics should not divide friends. You choose your candidate, and I choose my candidate, and whoever wins, wins, and then we go back to normal. It's no different than rooting for a sports team. You choose the team that you want to win, but you don't have to allow that to make you hostile and antagonistic toward people who support the other team.

But some people literally wanted me dead. They wanted to kill me; they wanted to ruin me. They wanted my church empty. They wanted my church shut down. If it was up to them, I would have wound up in the poorhouse or in the penitentiary.

My field of endeavor is Christianity. I've had talk shows on the radio where we debated everyday matters of faith. There are a lot of different beliefs within Christianity that are in opposition toward one another. You have the Calvinism school of thoughts versus the Arminian school of thought. You have different debates on water baptism and methods and different things like that. I've debated Muslims, Christian Scientists, Jehovah's Witnesses; I've debated Hindus, Buddhists, and every other different religion that you can think of. I've had all these debates. Political discourse is not my field of endeavor. I could read as well as the next person. Politics was a new venture for me in the realm of public discourse.

Trump got the support of the common man, the ordinary man—people such as me. It caused the "experts" to wonder, "Who are these people? Nobody knows who they are." But Trump knows the value of his brand, and the value of his name association. He looked at it as, "These people support me, and I'm going to give them a platform." Hillary wouldn't take an average, ordinary person and give him or her national notoriety. She went after celebrities and the like.

President-Elect Trump called me the day after Thanksgiving. I called him Mr. President for the first time and congratulated him. He was very humble.

He said, "Who'd have thought, huh?"

I said, "Ya know?"

* * *

The election victory was bittersweet for me, personally and professionally. A lot of my church members left over presidential politics. People were saying, "I'm leaving because of Donald Trump."

I would say, "How the heck are you leaving your church because of Donald Trump?"

I never endorsed him from my pulpit. I never talked about him in a sermon. I reserved that time and that platform for God. I always told my congregation: "I'm not going to tell you who to vote for. You vote with your conscience. I will vote with mine."

One person told me they were leaving the church because they were sick of fighting with their family. Family members were saying, "How can you go to that church? Your pastor is a sellout, your pastor is a race traitor. How can you go there?" Some were arguing at work, too, because they went to my church.

Then came the anonymous letters:

"Somebody needs to come over there and kill you."

"Somebody needs to shoot you."

"You'd better watch your back. You'd better watch yourself."

My reply was always, "Come on over here and do it, then."

They never came.

A segment in my church did stand by our side. My wife was preaching at a women's event at a church in the city. She went into the bathroom, and a little old lady was in there. This lady had to be in her eighties.

She said, "Hi, Pastor Belinda. I'm glad you're here. Don't let those people get you down, those ones that are criticizing you so much."

She opened up her purse and showed my wife a gun, and said, "I've got your back."

My wife and I both thought that was hilarious.

My men were coming to church with their firearms, too. They became very protective of me. I would say, "You don't have to do all of that. I don't need all of that." They'd say, "We're doing it anyway."

Thankfully, I never had an incident. And I didn't actually get much flak from Clevelanders; the death threats all came from outside Cleveland. Some people would talk smack on social media, but they know me in Cleveland. They know that I'm a confrontational type of guy.

Nobody ever came and tried to disrupt my church, although I heard that churches were being disrupted here and there. Bishop Wayne T. Jackson's church was disrupted after Trump was there.

Nobody ever came up in my church. Good thing they didn't. If people had come up here, they would have gotten dealt with. I'm serious. My guys don't play.

When people ran up in Bishop Jackson's church, one guy put a video of it out on social media. A guy in Cleveland reposted the video and wrote, "I heard they're going to Pastor Scott's church next."

I replied swiftly: "Why don't you come over here?"

He never responded.

Years ago, a Baptist church in Cleveland had Louis Farrakhan speak. I was very vociferous about that. I was doing my daily radio program, and I opened up the phone lines and harshly criticized the event. "You might as well offer a swine on the altar," I said. "You're going to have that anti-Christian demagogue come into a Christian church and speak? He's an enemy of the cross."

Some local Nation of Islam supporters heard me. About fifteen of them came up to my church in two minivans, saying: "We want to see Pastor Scott."

I came out, and about twenty-five of my guys surrounded them and said, "You better get in that car and get out of here if you know what's best for you."

They got back in their minivans and pulled off, and we never heard from them again.

* * *

When my wife was young, she was a Black Nationalist. In Cleveland, the Black Nationalists were like the Black Panthers. Belinda had her Black Nationalist name and wore army fatigues and stuff. She saw a guy shot dead during the riots. She witnessed tanks rolling down her streets.

She was very heavy into Black Nationalism back then.

When my friends and I were growing up in the sixties, we had Angela Davis posters on the wall. We had images of Martin Luther King Jr. and Eldridge Cleaver. If we walked past somebody, we'd give them the black power fist, and we had the Afros. I was very much in touch with my blackness during that time. Anybody who calls me a coon or an Uncle Tom doesn't know me.

In 2016 I told Don Lemon and Bakari Sellers, live on CNN: "When I was growing up in the sixties, the black unemployment rate was high. We couldn't get jobs. The black graduation rate was low. Black people were getting beat up by the police, and black people rioted in the streets."

I continued, "And here it is, 2016, and we're rioting in the streets. We're getting beat up by the police. Our unemployment rate is high, and our graduation rate is low—under Obama, the first black president. The same things that were going on when I was a kid in the sixties are going on now, with a black president that's been in office for eight years."

They couldn't argue.

I said, "I'm old enough to be most of you guys' father. The things you read about in the history books, I lived through. I experienced. What you guys know intellectually, I know experientially. Experiential knowledge is a whole lot different than intellectual knowledge."

You know intellectually that if you stick a bobby pin in a light socket, you're going to get shocked. You know intellectually that if you stick your hand in a fire, you're going to get burned. But until you know it experientially, you don't know it as deeply as you could.

I told them, "You young guys can't tell me anything about what it means to be black in America."

* * *

After the election, a lot of people wanted a share in the spoils of victory, as they should have. They wanted mainly jobs, positions, or appointments.

President-Elect Trump called me the day after Thanksgiving 2016.

After I congratulated him on the victory, he surprised me with a question. "What do you want?" he said.

"What do you mean, what do I want?"

"We won. What do you want? Do you want an appointment or something?"

I said, "No, I don't want anything. I don't want a job. I never wanted a job." I have a profession. I said, "I'm too old and set in my ways anyway. I'm a creature of habit. I like to get up when I get up, go to bed when I want, set my own schedule, be my own boss."

I continued, "However, what I do want is this. I want to be a conduit, a liaison, between the Trump administration and the black community."

Trump sounded a bit surprised. "You got it."

When there are issues pertaining to urban America, the inner cities, opportunity zones, prison reform, and other things like that, he invites me to sit at the table. He listens to my voice, and he allows me to give him advice. I find that very remarkable.

* * *

As surprising as it may sound, Trump takes advice from a lot of people who would surprise you.

I ran into Reince Priebus recently. I was busting his chops and calling him "Reese Primbus," like Don King had at the RNC. I love to bust people's chops.

"Where are you going?" I asked him.

He said, "I'm on my way up to the White House."

"I thought you got fired. What are you doing going over there?"

Priebus put on his professor hat. "You know what I learned? The people that have the best relationships with the president are the ones that don't work for him or the ones that used to work for him. The ones that have the problems are the ones that currently work for him, because the dynamics of the relationship change. When you don't work for him, you have a horizontal relationship. I mean, he's the president, you have to give him that respect. But when you do work for him, you have a vertical relationship. Some people take positions in the administration with Trump the friend or Trump the acquaintance. When he becomes Trump the boss, they don't like it."

That's why Trump has had the turnover that he's had. Some former staffers had a better relationship when they didn't work for him. Some get along with the president better now than when they were employees of the campaign or of the White House.

* * *

After the election, I was asked to participate in the National Prayer Service. There I met Ike Perlmutter, who has since become a good friend, and his wife, Laura. The president had mentioned Ike to me during the campaign, and Michael Cohen had put me on the phone with him. We were able to meet in person during the inauguration.

Ike's a great guy with a great personality. He's a very strong supporter of the president. I spent a lot of time with him and his wife, and love both of them.

The inauguration was the president's moment. I was glad for him. There were a lot of people there, but it was really his moment and his family's moment.

SEVEN

Racism can be very subtle, as I said earlier. Black people pick up on racist things that a lot of white people just don't see. We know what to look for. It can be just a glance. It can be a tone of voice.

I've seen no racism in Donald Trump, in public or in private. And in fact, I never experienced any racism, not even subtle, from anyone associated with the campaign. The racism that I experienced came from my own people. Black people called me derogatory, racist names: coon, Uncle Tom, sellout, Stepin Fetchit, Amos 'n' Andy, bootlicker, brown nose. Whatever derogatory name you can use for a black man, I heard it—from my own people.

But everybody I dealt with on the Trump campaign welcomed me with open arms. Everybody treated me the same as they treated everyone else. I walked in with my eyes open, trying to be as observant as I possibly could, to see if I could detect some racism there, but I never detected any, from anyone.

During the campaign, Trump was having a debate in Detroit. Since I am from Cleveland, my wife and I decided to go.

I talked to Omarosa about it. We had become pretty good friends by then. We're both from Ohio, and we're both black. I liked her personality. She's very volatile and outgoing, and I'm volatile and outgoing. She was always very pro-Trump and never said anything to me that disparaged him; she was always very protective of him.

She had a friend in Ohio who lived not too far from me in Seven Hills. She decided to fly to Ohio and then drive with her friend to Detroit. The debate was in Detroit's historical Fox Theatre.

Omarosa got there first and called us from inside. She said, "There's quite a long line outside, and the demonstrators and the protestors are out there. Make sure that you're careful."

It had been raining pretty badly in Detroit, but by the time we parked at the theater, the rain had stopped. We got out of the car and walked over. Some of the protestors were beating a drum in front of the theater, some were carrying signs, and some were chanting "Black Lives Matter." It was a carnival atmosphere out front. There was a police barricade and a rope across the front. Those on the theater side of the rope were going into the debate. Those on the other side were either spectating or protesting.

One of the ladies on the street side of the rope began to holler, "There's Trump's boy, there's Trump's boy right there. Hey, everybody, look! There's Trump's boy!"

She tried to point me out in the crowd. I popped my collar up and kept my head straight forward. I didn't want to be in Detroit fighting with a huge crowd of protestors. I tried to keep walking.

She kept hollering, "There's Trump's boy, y'all! Hey, right there, that's Trump's guy!"

A boldness came upon my wife, and she went right up to the lady.

She said, "Yeah, that's Trump's guy, and I'm his wife. Is there anything else you want to say? What are you trying to do? Get my husband killed? He's black just like you. What's the matter with you?"

She embarrassed the lady, who said, "Well, I'm sorry."

* * *

You have to understand, my wife is more sensitive than I am. God calls females the weaker of us, and that's speaking physically, because oftentimes women are stronger, especially black women. Strong females are a part of our culture. When I say she's more sensitive, I'm saying that she's more observant and keener than I am.

She's also much more creative. She's an artist; she was a singer. To be honest, the campaign took more of a toll on her than it did on me. It put a strain on our relationship at certain junctures, because she's not argumentative by nature. I am.

If she believes in something strongly, she's combative but not argumentative. She's able to defend her position or make her point with wisdom, astuteness, and common sense. She commands a room without being loud and demonstrative. She's very cultured, refined, and sophisticated. She's a lady. She's gracious.

Sometimes her greatest battle during all this was to hold her peace and not respond like I respond, because that would be out of character.

My daughter and grandchildren also had to go through it. They got into confrontations at school because people were calling their grandparents names. My daughter is much like her mother; she's not loud-mouthed or argumentative. She's a lady. She's gracious and mannerly, like my wife.

When people started boycotting us, we'd wake up every day and read all those attacks on our social media pages. People attacked my daughter's social media page and my grandkids' social media pages. It didn't bother me when they attacked mine, but for my wife to open up her social media page and read, "Your husband is a coon; your husband is an Uncle Tom"—or they called her a coon or an Uncle Tom or a sellout because she was married to me—that's an entirely different dynamic. I wish I could have done something about that.

Even though I would tell her, "Forget that, never mind that, don't pay attention to that," there were times she cried herself to sleep at night, and it affected a lot of our lives. It affected our relationship with church members who had been with us for years, members who said, "I'm leaving the church because of your support for Donald Trump." It was very disappointing that they would allow fake news to persuade them to leave the church, simply because of political leanings.

There are several businesses in our church facilities, as I mentioned. My daughter owns a boutique. We have a daycare business. We have office space and a banquet hall for rent. We own a radio station. There was a mass boycott of our church, the radio station, and any other businesses associated with our name. All my local advertisers and the local preachers and some national preachers who were on the radio station pulled out. The black community has a mob mentality sometimes. A lynch mob mentality as well. They wanted to hurt us because we supported Trump.

Our radio station had won a Stellar Award for large-market gospel radio station of the year. But during the boycott, people said: "Don't listen and don't advertise on that radio station."

"Don't patronize their banquet hall business," people also said. They didn't care that we have the best rates and one of the greatest facilities to have a banquet in the Greater Cleveland area. People boycotted everything that our name was attached to. The preachers applauded, because they hoped that the members who left our church would attend theirs.

We had to believe in God. I wasn't going to let anybody see me sweat. I've always had a strong faith in God. I told myself: *This is just another area for me to believe God in, or more things I'll have to believe in God for.*

But as I said, it caused strain in our lives sometimes, and I walked around with a certain measure of guilt. When I would come in and see seats empty in my church that used to be full; when I would see the numbers drop at the daycare; when I would see a lot of people I was formerly in a relationship with talking about me and criticizing me over the internet and social media; when smear campaigns were leveled against me and fake news was published about me, it could be disheartening. But I don't have the type of personality that gets depressed. I don't get depressed; I get pissed. I get angry. It fuels me and motivates me to dig in deeper, and to try harder.

* * *

One Saturday morning, Michael Cohen and I were talking. He was upset. The racist narrative being used against Donald Trump was irritating and agitating him. It bothered him that the media was playing the race card.

"The boss is not a racist," he said. "Believe me, I know him. I've been with him. I'm the son of a Holocaust survivor. I wouldn't be with a guy that was a racist."

Cohen continued, "I wish we could come up with some type of organization, or coalition, of like-minded black people, African Americans, who don't mind publicly supporting Donald Trump, because this narrative in the media portraying him as a racist is a false narrative."

He went on to talk about the fact that not only was Trump *not* a racist, but Trump actually was very proactive concerning black people, and was planning to be even more so if elected.

I said, " Let me think about it. I'll pray about it, and we'll come up with something tomorrow."

We talked the next day. "Listen, I thought about it," I said, "and I think that instead of having a coalition of African Americans, we want an organization that will be inclusive and not exclusive. Why don't we say 'diversity'?"

We settled on National Diversity Coalition for Trump, or NDC Trump. It had a good ring to it.

I contacted Bruce LeVell, with whom I'd become very close during the campaign. He and I were more or less free agents who were friends of the campaign. We didn't have an official position—we worked with the campaign but not *for* it.

I shared the idea with Bruce, and he loved it. We contacted Omarosa as well, and she loved it, too. We would set it up as a volunteer organization. We agreed that Michael Cohen and I would be co-CEOs. We selected Bruce as our executive director, which I think was a very good choice, because he's very aggressive. He's been with the Republican Party for decades, and he knows a lot of people. He's a great communicator, and he's a people person.

Every day, people joined the coalition, and it was an amazing thing. We had my friend Jesse Singh, who led Sikh Americans for Trump. Wayne Dupree came along; he was named 2015 Blogger of the Year by the American Conservative Union. Sajid "CJ" Tarar, Muslim Americans for Trump. We had Puerto Ricans for Trump, Pakistanis for Trump, Colombians for Trump, and Haitians for Trump. Stephanie Mendoza Hamill and Carlos Limón came on board, representing Mexicans for Trump.

We had supporters of all kinds from all over America: Jewish, Korean, Chinese, Filipino, Latino, Cuban, Portuguese, Persian, South African, Indian, Japanese, Vietnamese, Bulgarian, and Polish people. National Black Pro-Life Union president Dr. Day Gardner came on board. Steve Parson joined as an African-American pastor for Trump.

Our ranks swelled. We even had Millennials for Trump and Small Business for Trump. Pastor Eric Cowley came on board, and he had hundreds of pastors representing hundreds of thousands of members who all wanted to be a part of the National Diversity Coalition for Trump. It was a wonderful thing. Greek-American millennial entrepreneur Christos Marafatsos came on board. It was just a melting pot, a smorgasbord of Trump supporters.

We hit the ground running, and Michael Cohen and I were both very proud of the NDC. That's one of the reasons I was disappointed when, during those congressional hearings, Cohen stood up and accused the president of racism.

They got to Cohen. Broke him.

I can't say what I would or would not have done if I had been in his shoes. Being from the streets, I have a different mindset. We had a code in the streets of not bending or breaking for the authorities. That's something that's in me and in the black community as well. People from the urban communities and inner cities don't turn on friends because they're in a jam with the law, even though I've known people who have been turned and broken.

Like Cohen.

* * *

One day shortly before the election, Cohen called me on the phone.

He said, "Are you watching the news?"

I said no.

He said, "Turn the news on."

The news was claiming that Michael Cohen said that he paid money to porn actress Stormy Daniels as "hush money." Daniels was alleging that she had an affair with Trump.

I said, "Wow, man, what did you do that for? Why did you tell them that you paid money? What happened?"

He replied: "I said, 'Fuck it.'"

"What?"

"I said, 'Fuck it.'"

Cohen texted me a video of the Muppets singing, "I said, 'Fuck it.'"

I didn't talk about it after that. I never asked him whether or not Trump had had an affair with Stormy Daniels, because I didn't want to know. Cohen came out with his statement on the subject, seemingly out of the blue. I think he was seeking Trump's approval by doing that.

Over time, he began to get bitter, possibly because he didn't get the response from Trump that he was seeking.

In 2017, after a televised event at the White House's Rose Garden, Cohen called me again. He said, "What are you up to? Were you at the Rose Garden event?"

"Yes," I replied. "I'm on my way to CNN."

"Well, what are you going on there to talk about?"

"Today's event," I responded.

He said, "When you go on, this is what you should say. You should say, 'Michael Cohen is a great guy.' You should say that Michael Cohen is getting a raw deal."

I thought, *They're not bringing me on to advocate for Michael Cohen.* But I didn't say that to him. I told him I would see what I could do.

He went on to complain very angrily about how everyone was enjoying the president's victory except for him. Everybody was reaping a harvest for their labor except for him. Everyone was enjoying the spoils of victory except for him.

He complained that a lot of people were at the Rose Garden event, but he wasn't. He complained about being in a hotel, unable to go outside because of the media. He complained about how other people had positions in the White House, but he didn't. He started getting digs in on the president, saying derogatory things that I had never heard him say before.

He didn't mention that he was getting millions of dollars from companies for "consulting," because of his proximity to Trump.

I began to feel very uncomfortable with the tone of our conversation. He had become a very bitter man.

I didn't have a chance to warn the president about him. I didn't see him until after it all hit the fan. However, I saw Don Jr. in New York soon after that conversation, and I told him, "I'm having a bad feeling about Cohen. I think he's going to turn. Let your father know what I said."

Everybody knew how close Cohen and I were, and for him to turn like that, frankly, was very disappointing.

The president and I had one very brief conversation about Cohen after that. It was in private, in the Oval Office after a meeting at the White House, and the conversation consisted of five words.

He looked at me and said, "Can you believe that guy?"

I didn't have to ask, "What guy?" We both knew who he was talking about. I just shook my head. Then we moved on.

He didn't talk bad about Cohen to me, and I didn't talk bad about Cohen to him. We both shared a mutual understanding and a mutual disappointment.

* * *

In the summer of 2018, Cohen began to be openly hostile. During our conversations, he started saying things like, "Well, this guy should have never been president in the first place." I was astounded when he said that. I felt I had no choice but to cut this guy off. I stopped taking his calls, because I didn't trust him anymore.

When I was out in the streets, there was a mindset that everyone understood. If a guy got arrested or caught a case, he became "hot." When a guy was hot, it didn't matter how much you liked him or even if he was your family member; you couldn't associate with him. I didn't trust Cohen anymore; he was hot. Not only was he hot, but he was also being a snitch. And the snitching was not even based upon facts—it was based upon feelings.

At that time, Cohen was removed from the NDC website. He wanted to know why he had been removed. We told him, "With your opposition towards the President, your open hostility and charges of racism, we had no choice but to remove you." This was the National Diversity Coalition for Trump, not against Trump. He didn't like it, but there was nothing he could do about it. I believe he would rather have had the entire organization disband, which wasn't going to happen.

In 2019, Cohen began testifying before Congress regarding the "investigation" into Russian interference in the 2016 presidential election. I talked with someone in Congressman Mark Meadows's office, who said, "We want to know if you would be willing to come and render any testimony that could help."

I said, "Well, there's nothing I can add that would help us, simply because there were certain things that Cohen didn't talk to me about."

Cohen never directly told me any of the things he said the president did. I think we had the type of relationship that if those things did indeed happen, he would have told me.

When I watched Michael Cohen on television testify under oath that he did not want a job at the White House, that he had never solicited a job at the White House, that he had never been interested in a job at the White House, I couldn't take it anymore.

I had to tweet that he was lying. I couldn't just sit there, because if he was lying about that, what else was he lying about? I tweeted that he had asked me on several occasions to try to help him get a job at the White House, which he had. Congressman Meadows saw the tweet, and it was read on live television during the hearings and entered into the *Congressional Record.* I'll never forget the look on Cohen's face when the tweet was read. He kind of slumped imperceptibly, his jaw dropped, and there was a look on his face of utter resignation, because he knew that he had repeatedly asked me to try to help him get a position in the White House. I felt sorry for him for maybe a millisecond, but then I didn't, because he was flat-out lying.

Cohen would always ask me, "Did you see the boss?"

I'd say, "I saw him."

"Did he ask about me?"

"Yeah, he asked about you."

"Well, what did he say?"

"He asked how you were doing."

"What did you say?"

"I told him you were doing fine. I told him you were doing this and you were doing that."

"He's going to have an event. When you see him, he's going to ask about me. When he asks about me, tell him that he should bring me up to the White House. Tell him that he should give me a job. Tell him that Michael is the only one that can watch his back. Tell him that I should be chief of staff."

I'd be sitting there saying to myself, *I'm not telling him all of that.*

Once during the campaign, when Trump and I were riding in a car together, he asked me, "Have you talked to Michael lately?"

"Yeah, I talked to him earlier today," I said.

"What's he up to?"

"He was engaged in a Twitter war with Mark Cuban."

The president said, "About what?"

"About you."

"Oh yeah? Get him on the phone," Trump said.

I got Cohen on the phone, and I said, "The boss wants to speak to you."

He got on the phone, and Trump said, "I heard you were involved in a Twitter war with Mark Cuban. You know what? I've got all of these emails from Mark Cuban, cozying up to me, because he wanted me to let him be a part of this campaign or whatever." He continued, "I never responded to it, and that's why he's mad at me. I'll tell you what. You want to have some fun with him on Twitter?"

"Yeah," said Cohen.

"Tell him that he's got a weak golf swing," Trump said.

Trump always had a concern for Michael Cohen. He was genuinely surprised when Cohen flipped like he did.

* * *

The National Diversity Coalition provided a platform for a number of people to engage during the campaign. It gave them unofficial campaign positions.

It pleased me a lot when I would see different members of the coalition on television, and on the lower third of the screen their position in the National Diversity Coalition would be noted. I appreciated that very much because the NDC became, and still remains, a very influential organization that people want to be a part of.

Because NDC Trump is a volunteer-based organization, no demands are placed upon people in it. Lillie Ramos Pozatek, a Colombian American, joined, and she's been a great help in keeping us connected, notified of different events, and in communication with one another via email. It takes a tremendous load off me as the CEO. The members of the NDC do a lot of work that they don't get recognition for, and I want to thank them.

The campaign began to rely on the NDC. I realized its value more and more during the course of the campaign. When candidate Trump was levied with charges of racism, among other things, the campaign relied upon the NDC to send supporters out who would advocate on his behalf.

We became a storehouse for the campaign. If certain ethnic groups were needed to advocate for Trump or write op-eds, we had them. We had the resources available for people who were ready, willing, able, and very capable of defending this president.

I find it ironic that the National Diversity Coalition was basically Michael Cohen's brainchild. He and I gave birth to it together, but the original idea came from him. For him, a year or two later, to levy charges of racism against the president was flabbergasting. I believe one of the reasons no one took his accusations seriously was that they knew he was an architect of the NDC, and it made him appear very hypocritical.

It saddens me to see Cohen in prison, but once he began to express open hostility toward the president, I had to disconnect. Prior to that, he would cry on my shoulder somewhat, and I maintained communication with him because I would try to be a mediator. I tried to assuage those feelings he had. Being a pastor and having counseled people for decades, I have experience in comforting, mediating, and soothing hurt feelings.

But I couldn't get involved to the point where I allowed Cohen's feelings about Trump to change my own feelings about Trump. The issues that arose between Cohen and Trump were personal, and it's very unfortunate what happened between them. But once Cohen's hostility became public, it became time for me to draw a line, to choose sides. It wasn't difficult, because Cohen was not the reason for my relationship with Trump. On the contrary, Trump was the reason for my relationship with Cohen. The unifying factor. The glue of the relationship. If Donald Trump had not run for president, I would have never known Michael Cohen. The thing that united us was our common interest in Trump's becoming president.

* * *

One thing that I think I've been pretty good at doing, because it was impressed upon me in the early days of my Christianity, is suppressing my ego. In Christianity, we call it the flesh. We don't want our flesh to get control of us; we don't want our egos to take over and dominate our actions.

A lot of people who worked with the campaign began believing their own press clippings. They appeared on television and began to think of themselves as journalists, pundits, or media correspondents. You could see it on their social media platforms, things like "as seen on Fox" (or CNN or MSNBC). They began to think they were more than what they really were.

When you look back at the 2016 campaign, you can see that other candidates tried to get as much star power as they could. Hillary Clinton came to my city, Cleveland, and had an event with Beyoncé, Jay-Z, and LeBron James, which didn't fill even half the auditorium. Hollywood actors and actresses would associate with different candidates, like Bernie Sanders or Hillary Clinton, attempting to use their star power to garner support for them.

Trump doesn't do that. He doesn't need to go after entertainers, athletes, and actors, to add a bump to his campaign or to attract an audience he doesn't already have. He fills arenas by himself. It's unprecedented. I've never seen anything like it in politics. He's a star maker, and anyone who stands next to him or walks alongside him automatically becomes a media personality.

But some people fail to realize that they're only a media personality because of their relationship with and proximity to him. Once, when my business partner Kareem Lanier and I were meeting with bankers and developers regarding our urban revitalization initiative, one executive with a major national developer told us, "I can get you more support for this if you disconnect from Trump."

I said, "You sound like a fool. Without Trump, all we are is two more black guys with a plan. The reason you let us in this room with you now is because you know me from my association with Trump." We got up and walked out, leaving those executives sitting there, speechless. We didn't straighten our chairs up, either.

Trump made media personalities of a lot of people—such as me, Diamond and Silk, Bruce LeVell, and Mark Burns—because of our proximity to him and the fact that he allowed us to speak on his behalf. He made us public figures.

When the campaign ended, I began working with the administration, doing what I could to help advance its policies in this country, especially regarding the black community. I was advocating for and endeavoring to advance the cause of African Americans, while still utilizing the National Diversity Coalition as a liaison between the administration and those who represented their particular ethnic groups.

We continue that even now, meaning I'm just as busy now as I was during the campaign, making media appearances for whatever reason the president allows.

* * *

Fame is relative. During the campaign, one preacher recommended that Trump go to T. D. Jakes's church. He's an icon in the black community.

Paul Manafort said, "Who is that?"

An entire world out there is not familiar with the "celebrities" of the Black Church community. It made me realize how significant or insignificant some people are in the grand scheme of things. One person's big is another person's small. But the presidency of the United States is the biggest platform in the world. It doesn't get any bigger than that.

Whoever is president is the biggest celebrity, personality, personage on the planet.

* * *

Someone once told me, "I can't think of any other black pastor in the history of this country that has ever had the type of friendship and relationship with the sitting president of the United States like you have."

I thought all the way back to George Washington. I said, "I know past presidents have had relationships with black pastors. But I don't know the depth of the friendships that they had."

I value President Trump's friendship. I don't make demands on it. I don't have any ulterior motives; I'm not trying to use him for gain. I met the guy, and I liked the guy. Our personalities are very similar. We both shoot from the hip. He talks smack; I talk smack. He doesn't take crap; I don't take crap.

* * *

Omarosa resigned from the National Diversity Coalition after receiving a job in the administration, which I'm happy about in hindsight.

Omarosa was very close with Trump. She campaigned very aggressively for a position in the White House. The president looked out for her. He rewarded her with a position that she didn't necessarily earn.

I remember her calling me and saying, "I got the job." She was excited. She had an office bigger than anybody else's. She had her own secretary. President Trump had appointed her the director of African-American outreach. He gave her a lot of liberty with that position as well.

President Trump gave Omarosa the ability to serve this country and advocate for the black community, in a position that was tailor-made for her, but it didn't last long.

After Star Jones left *The View*, she said: " I didn't realize until it was over that that position I had on *The View* was a gift." Omarosa didn't realize that Trump had given her a gift. I think she didn't value it until she didn't have it anymore.

Omarosa was concerned about the Mueller investigation. She wasn't thrilled about the possibility of being interrogated for hours or days by Mueller.

I replaced Omarosa on the board of the NDC, with Christos Marafatsos. In hindsight, I'm glad she resigned, because it saved me the job of having to remove her from the coalition or having her quit under different circumstances, once she became antagonistic toward this presidency.

Some people have never been in positions of leadership where they had to make difficult decisions. Sometimes leaders have to override or ignore personal feelings and make changes, or make unpopular decisions. Those who aren't leaders don't realize how difficult it is sometimes.

I don't think it was an easy decision for the president to agree to her firing, but it was a necessary one. And then Omarosa allowed her personal feelings to determine her response to the firing. She was removed from a position that she told me she was going to leave anyway. Why would she become upset when she was asked to resign?

She was offered a position within the reelection campaign. She would have received the same pay. She would have still had a lot of influence, as well as much more freedom and much less scrutiny. She would have still had access to the president, and their friendship would have been intact.

Omarosa began to play the race card, like Cohen had, after having defended Trump so vociferously during the campaign. That somewhat tarnished her testimony and impugned her credibility.

It would have been different if Cohen and Omarosa had said, "Well, originally, I didn't think he was this or that way, but I came to find out over the course of the campaign that he was." But there they were, the main ones who had defended Trump against allegations of racism, both having known and associated with him for years, accusing him of being a racist and saying, "Oh, we knew he was a racist the entire time."

That didn't fly with the American public. It left both of them without any type of base or support. You have to understand—those on the right rejected Omarosa and Cohen because they abandoned their support of Trump and, by extension, abandoned their support of the right and of conservatism.

The left didn't embrace them either. The Democratic Party and the left-wing media used them to further their agenda against Trump, and after they couldn't use them anymore, they discarded them.

Now they're people without a platform on either side.

* * *

It was very disappointing to find out that during the entire campaign, Omarosa had ulterior motives. I don't know if she was taping private conversations to protect herself, to use in her book, or for other reasons. She was very good at concealing that. During and after the campaign, and into Trump's presidency, I never heard her say one negative thing about Trump or any of the others. She always defended Trump in public and in private, and was very protective of him.

It reminded me a lot of Michael Cohen. The two of them seemed to have the same type of spirit. But they were protective to the detriment of Trump rather than to his benefit. I believe she acted out of hurt. I believe that she felt he should have not allowed her to be fired. She felt that President Trump should have defended her as strongly as she always defended him—ride or die, sink or swim, through hell or high water.

What I find somewhat puzzling is that Omarosa had told me in private that she was considering leaving the White House anyway. She said, "I'm going to be here another year, then I'm out."

The only reason she didn't leave earlier, she said, was because she was concerned that if she left the White House, she would be subpoenaed by the Mueller investigation. As long as she was an employee, she had some type of immunity.

I don't blame her for not wanting to be subpoenaed. She saw what they had done to General Flynn, Paul Manafort, Michael Cohen, and others. It was a modern-day inquisition, a very grueling experience. However, she had indicated that she wasn't planning to be at the White House through the full term anyway.

When she got let go, I was surprised by her reaction. I talked to her immediately after that, and she told me that she was very disappointed in the way she had been treated. She said they sequestered her in a room and treated her very harshly.

I used to hear a lot of rumblings about how Omarosa was very challenging, bold, assertive, and confrontational while she was in the White House, and how she didn't take any flak from anybody. Some accused her of being a bully. She made a lot of enemies during her tenure—at least behind her back, because a lot of people in the White House were afraid of her.

I will say this, though: She went to bat for me. She made it a point to make sure I was included in all the things that had to do with the African-American community. She made sure that I was there, that I had a seat at the table, and that I had VIP access.

I was in the Oval Office with the president soon after she got fired, and he asked me, "Have you talked to Omarosa?" He was still concerned about her.

"Yeah, I talked to her."

"Well, how's she doing?" Trump asked.

"She's doing alright," I said. "She's going to write a book."

"A book? What kind of book?"

"I guess some kind of memoir about her time on the campaign and in the administration."

He called out to Madeleine Westerhout, his secretary, in the lobby: "Madeleine, who's our best lawyer? Get our best lawyer on the phone, and tell them to get Omarosa on the phone, and tell her that if she writes some type of book, I'm going to sue her for the rest of her life."

Or something to that effect.

Madeleine said, "Well, I think she already knows that, sir."

"Well, get her on the phone and tell her again." Then he looked back at me and said, "You know we've got a nondisclosure agreement."

He added: "I defended her a lot, but a lot of people don't like her."

I said, "Yeah, I know."

"You know who doesn't like her the most?"

"Who?" I said.

"African Americans," Trump said.

I cracked up. We both had a good laugh.

I said, "I think you're right there."

He looked at me and said, "This is, like, my fourth time firing her."

I know he was very fond of her, and I believe that she was very fond of him. I believe she thinks he should have protected her more, but she didn't understand his position as the president. She was pretty disruptive. I know beyond a shadow of a doubt that if he did agree for her to be fired, it was a reluctant agreement.

One thing I always say is, mad wears off. Anger wears off. I wouldn't be surprised if sometime in the future Trump and Omarosa reconcile. They have a lot of positive history with each other, and they had a great relationship. No one advocated for Omarosa more than Donald Trump, and no one advocated for Donald Trump more than Omarosa.

Since the release of her book, we haven't talked. There's no animosity there, though. She understands politics very well. You have to choose sides, at least publicly. I have to be focused on what I'm doing.

I was disappointed when she wrote her book, even though she didn't say anything negative about me. I was disappointed more that she had taped some of the others and had used the tapes. Maybe she felt that she had to protect herself. Maybe it was all a part of her master plan. I don't know. Only she and God know.

* * *

The National Diversity Coalition was, and still is, a very viable entity for this country. It does a lot of work on behalf of different communities and different ethnicities. It has access to this administration that is used for good. We're planning even greater things going forward, to help enhance the quality of living for all Americans.

The president acknowledges, recognizes, receives, and appreciates the National Diversity Coalition for Trump. He endeavors to serve this organization to the best of his ability, even as we in this organization endeavor to serve him to the best of our ability as well.

A number of people have taken a lot of heat from their communities for their membership and participation in the NDC. I salute and applaud all of them for continuing as members in spite of that.

EIGHT

Pastor Mark Burns once said to me, "Black people supporting Hillary doesn't make news. Black people supporting Donald Trump does."

The Bible says people shouldn't think higher of themselves than they ought to, and I don't think higher of myself than I ought to. I've prevented myself from being bitten by the celebrity bug and getting caught up in my own press clippings and beginning to think that I'm more important or more significant than I am. I haven't begun to delude myself into believing that I'm some type of political pundit, journalist, news reporter, or commentator.

I'm just a pastor who, because of my proximity to Donald Trump and the fact that I am black, has a voice that has gained a certain level of significance. I understand that I'm usually called upon by the media to weigh in when it's something that concerns the black community, and I have no problem with that.

Once, I said to producers at CNN and at Fox, in a somewhat stern voice, "You guys only call me in when it's something about black people; why don't you call me in when it's about the economy? You don't call for my opinion on foreign policy and different things like that."

They got a little nervous, because they couldn't tell if I was serious or not. They didn't know I was just busting their chops. I said it half-jokingly, because they don't call economists or foreign policy advisors in to weigh in on black issues. I have no problem with that.

I also don't have a problem with the way President Trump utilizes those who are part of his board of surrogates or his team.

I understand that, as a developer he tends to compartmentalize his employees. As a developer, he'll put the electricians in one box, and he'll put the plasterers in another box. The drywall guys over here, and the plumbers over there. He'll deal with the plumbers when there's an issue with the plumbing. He'll deal with the electricians when there's an issue with the electricity.

He is the general contractor; he has to oversee it all. But he deals with, deploys, and utilizes those whose strengths are necessary for whatever the task at hand is. He has a cadre. He has teammates who are black, whom he can utilize when there are issues that affect or impact or require input from the black community.

We at the NDC are the ones he relies upon for advice in areas like that. He's the first one to admit that he does not have a total grasp of the intricacies and nuances of the black community, no more than I'm acquainted with the intricacies and nuances of the Mexican, Irish, Polish, German, or any other community. But Trump's detractors are going to try to find something wrong with him no matter what.

I learned to be a quick study. I learned the hard way that when I went into the lion's den, especially on CNN or MSNBC, my best defense was a strong offense. I read the news like anyone else, and I form my own conclusions or opinions, but I never wanted a new career as a political pundit. I try to keep up on current events more than I did in the past, because I never know when I'm going to be called to comment on something because of my relationship with President Trump.

I try to pride myself on being myself—on not getting caught up in the hype and being phony. I don't try to articulate in ways that are outside my normal way of articulation. I stopped wearing neckties a long time ago, because when I would preach, I would sweat. I would always wind up trying to loosen my tie to help me preach better. Many times, I would wind up breaking the top button off my shirt while trying to unbutton the shirt. As a result, I just don't wear neckties.

I'm comfortable enough with myself to go in public and remain the way that I am in private. Years ago I read something that impacted the way I thought. I was reading a story on Russell Simmons and on his rise in the corporate world to become one of the first black multimillionaires out of the hip-hop community.

The story told of how Simmons went into a boardroom to sit down and talk with some corporate executives. He wore jeans and Adidas sneakers, and he kept his hat turned to the back. He didn't put on a suit and a tie and present himself in a different way. Simmons was being himself, and that's what I try to do, be myself at all times. Love me or hate me.

It's hard for me to be phony. I learned that on CNN, I had to be somewhat irreverent to the people on set with me, because if I wasn't, they would try to take advantage of me. I found it humorous that in the green room, in the back, when the cameras were off, most of these people from the other side of the political spectrum were nice and friendly. Or soft. They would try to convince me that I was their friend, and when the cameras came on, they would try to rip me to shreds. I would be just as irreverent and intentionally disrespectful in private as I was in public, just to let them know not to mess with me.

As I mentioned, the left-wing networks would always try to get blacks fighting against blacks. The white program hosts and contributors were much more respectful to me than the black hosts and contributors. They were much more civil, less insulting, more careful in their interactions. I guess they felt that the black ones could say insulting things to me that they couldn't, and they wouldn't have to worry about being accused of being racists.

The black commentators would say things like, "I'm not part of your congregation. You don't have me fooled." They would be disrespectful and offensive. Whereas the white ones—Anderson Cooper, Erin Burnett, Brooke Baldwin—would try to be civil and respectful while we were on the air. The black ones would come on with an attitude like, "I ain't afraid of him. I'll get on there and tell him off."

Some were hostile toward me before we even had a chance. Maybe they'd seen me and just said to themselves, "Well, he ain't going to talk to me like that." They don't realize how amusing it was to me. I didn't care. As I've said before, I don't mind arguing or getting disrespectful. I would go back hard at them, male or female, and some would try to retreat into victimhood or accuse me of being a misogynist or something, simply because I wouldn't take their guff. They didn't understand how I could be pro-Trump without being anti-black.

I was never anti-black. I was actually more pro-black than they were, because I was trying to let black people see that it is okay to reject the party line, to walk to the beat of a different drum, to think for yourself, think outside the box. It's okay to go against the grain and defy conventional logic. They should have appreciated and applauded that, but they didn't, because it threatened their status quo. It made them feel uncomfortable.

Trump would rather have somebody be upfront, honest, and direct in disagreement than to be untruthful and indirect in agreement.

We were able to strategize and formulate a campaign strategy revolving around the African-American community without anyone's feeling uncomfortable. Now I've already told you a little bit about our trip to Bishop Wayne T. Jackson's church in Detroit, but here's more of the story. I wasn't involved in arranging the meeting, other than being a character reference for the bishop, whom I'd been friends with for years. When the campaign asked me if I knew him, I said I thought his church would be a good place to visit. Bishop Jackson owned the Impact Network, the largest African American–owned gospel network in the country.

He agreed to host candidate Trump at his church, and since it was only a three-hour drive from where I lived, I decided to go there with him. Omarosa came with him too, and I took a couple of people with me. When we got there, there were protestors outside, but not a lot. Their voices were heard, but the protestors didn't resort to violence or try to disrupt the meeting.

Bishop Jackson took Trump back to interview him for his television program, and that caused some confrontation early on. Not between Trump and Bishop Jackson; they got along famously.

The confrontation was over the fact that Omarosa wanted to be in the room as well. For whatever reason, she felt that she had to "protect" Trump from black people. I didn't understand that then or now.

Omarosa and Bishop Jackson did not hit it off at all. Trump thought he was going to speak, and had some notes prepared in his pocket. Bishop Jackson didn't know that he was planning to speak. Omarosa and Bishop Jackson got into an argument.

I was the man in the middle. Bishop Jackson came to me and said, "You'd better get her. You'd better talk to her."

I said, "Okay, I'll talk to her."

Meanwhile, Omarosa came to me and said, "You'd better get him. You'd better talk to him."

I said, "Okay, I'll talk to him."

I found myself trying to be the mediator. Omarosa was insisting that Trump should speak. Bishop Jackson was adamant that Trump would not speak. He wasn't prepared for him to speak. He was very selective over whom he allowed in his pulpit, which was his prerogative. He had thought that Trump was just coming to visit, that they would interview him in the back and then Trump would listen to him preach, like so many other politicians had done in his church in the past.

Trump calmed Omarosa down. He said, "No, that's alright. I don't have to speak. It's his church. If he doesn't want me to speak, I don't have a problem with it." He put his notes back in his pocket.

He was not going to leave, as some claimed. He wasn't upset. He had no animosity or hostility. I was right there. I witnessed the entire thing. He understood and recognized authority. He understood and recognized that Bishop Jackson was the leader of that church.

Trump has always had a high regard for the clergy, for preachers. Whenever he's in the room with preachers, he adopts the position of the lesser and looks at the preachers as the greater.

I guess when Trump said he didn't have to speak, it touched Bishop Jackson's heart. The bishop said, "No, that's alright. He can speak."

Trump delivered his prepared speech, and it was warmly received by those in attendance. Bishop Jackson then delivered his sermon, and his wife, who is an amazing singer, sang. Trump was very impressed with her talent.

After the service but before the dismissal, Bishop Jackson presented Trump with some parting gifts: a Bible and a Jewish prayer shawl. While the gifts were being given, Omarosa went up onstage to stand behind Trump. She made sure that she was in the picture, which I thought was funny. Trump had a great time.

Afterward, as I mentioned previously, we were going to Ben Carson's family home, and Trump said, "Come on, ride in the car with me." Also in the car were James Davis (one of my co-pastors), Steve Bannon, Dave Bossie, and Keith Schiller.

Trump said, "Wow, that was a great service." He had his Bible and prayer shawl with him. "His wife can really sing, can't she?"

I said, "People from Detroit can sing before they can walk."

He said of Bishop Jackson, "Wow, that guy has a great smile. I like him a lot."

I don't know how many Black Church services Trump has been in, coming out of the evangelical world. Evangelical services are kind of reserved and subdued, but Black Church services are lively. He enjoyed himself. He enjoyed the singing, the preaching, the fellowship. We pulled away in the car, and by that time, the crowd of protestors had shrunk to around three or four guys.

* * *

Over at Ben Carson's house, Carson and Trump had a press conference. Trump got out of the car, and Keith Schiller, Dave Bossie, James Davis, and I moved to the background. Omarosa, on the other hand, tried her best to make sure she was before the camera at all times.

We said, "Look at her. She just has to get in the picture." We weren't surprised, though. We just shook our heads and laughed.

* * *

I once asked myself how I would respond if someone said I didn't like white people. I would say, "There are some white people I don't like. There are a lot of white people I do like. But as far as me hating the white race...no, I don't hate the white race. I don't hate any race."

I wouldn't try to start acting stereotypically white. I wouldn't change my voice and mannerisms to "act white" when I got around white people. I wouldn't begin to pander to convince white people that I wasn't a racist. What a lot of people don't like about Trump is that he would never get out of character and pander to the black community. And a lot of the black leaders don't like it because if he did that, they would be able to criticize him for it.

If I were him, I would have done the same thing. I would simply state my position and not try to overemphasize the fact that I'm not against any particular race. I would just continue to do what I've normally done.

Trump looks at the black community just like he looks at any other community. They're people. He looks at the human community and the American community.

* * *

We had a great time in Detroit, and the meeting at the church was a home run. We all had good conversation afterward. Trump still considers Bishop Jackson a friend. It disappointed me a little that the bishop would never come out in public and say that he was a Trump supporter.

There was some blowback at the bishop's church later. Anti-Trumpers in the community sent in some rabble-rousers who tried to disrupt his service, and Bishop Jackson was definitely impacted by it.

* * *

A lot of my fellow pastors told me in private that they were afraid: "I don't have the courage you have. I don't have the boldness that you have."

I would tell them, "I don't have any extreme amount of courage or boldness that no one else has; I just have to be true to myself. I either believe God or don't believe God. I either trust Him to keep me or don't trust Him."

People would say, "I don't know how you did it."

"Did what?"

"Stand up under all of that pressure."

"What pressure?"

"Everyone attacking you and criticizing you."

I would reply, "That's not pressure. Pressure is if I've got five children and a wife, and no income, and someone at home is sick with a disease that's unto death. Pressure is getting evicted after getting your home foreclosed on. Pressure is getting put out on the sidewalk in three days and you don't have anywhere to go. Pressure is when your kids are hungry and you can't pay your bills. That's pressure. Somebody talking about me or somebody criticizing me on social media isn't pressure. I can control that. All I have to do is not look at it. All I have to do is not read it. If it bothers me, I don't read it. If I can't stomach it, I don't look at it."

If your perception of pressure is public opinion, you can forget it. People talking badly about me, what is that? If you consider yourself a leader, you have to lead, regardless of public opinion, and stay true to your convictions to the best of your ability.

NINE

Every two to four years, Democrats play the game, as my friend Pastor James Davis calls it, "Pin the Racist on the Republican." They called George W. Bush a racist. They said that John McCain was a racist. They said that Mitt Romney was a racist. Every two to four years, racism is trotted out as a Republican demerit and as a Democratic talking point.

Republican policies are more favorable to the people, to the man on the street, than Democratic policies. The Democratic Party did not give the black or Latino community or women one intellectual reason not to support Donald Trump. They gave emotional reasons. They told the Latinos and blacks, "Trump hates you, and because he hates you, don't vote for him." They told women that he's a misogynist and sexist: "He oppresses you, and he looks at you as being inferior. Don't vote for him."

The Democrats offer the people handouts; the Republicans offer the people a hand up. There's a difference: a handout promotes dependence, while a hand up promotes independence.

Both result in a certain mindset. People with an independent mindset think for themselves—oftentimes outside the box. They are able to process information and come to their own conclusions. Democrats want to continue the handouts in order to control an entire community, an entire voting bloc, through controlling people's minds via a mindset of dependency.

A lot of black people have a handout mentality. They want government handouts. That's why, even as I write this in the 2020 election cycle, they talk about everything being free, even though they know that nothing in life is free. It's a total falsehood.

When President Trump criticized Congressman Elijah Cummings's district in Baltimore in 2019, the media interviewed a woman who agreed with the criticism. I found it remarkable that in her critique, the woman criticizing Cummings did not say one negative thing about the horrible condition of her community. She said nothing about the blighted housing, run-down slums, rats, or garbage.

She said, "Elijah Cummings hasn't done anything. He hasn't had a book bag giveaway, and we haven't had any cookouts."

The president was criticizing the physical condition of her community based on how blighted and run-down it had become. The woman, on the other hand, was judging Cummings's job success, or failure, by what he had not given them. If Cummings had given out free book bags and had a cookout for the community, then he would have been alright in the mind of that woman and others. But because he hadn't given out anything, he wasn't considered good, and that's a mindset.

When Democratic politicians go into the white community, they have town hall meetings, public forums, and roundtables to connect and communicate with the white community. But oftentimes when they go into the black community, they go to a cookout, concert, church, or dance. They have videos taken of them dancing or eating fried chicken or other "black food." It's an entirely different dynamic, and that's because the Democratic Party perceives us in a different way.

President Trump was criticized because he came along in the midst of this mindset and said, "What do you have to lose?"

The media went bonkers and tried to misconstrue his intentions. They acted like he had said something racist and negative. The black community was incensed, too: "Trump's insulting us." "He's racist; he made a racist statement." "He's looking down on us."

When President Trump asked, "What do you have to lose?" he meant, "Give me a chance. Give me a shot! The worst that can happen is that I don't do anything. The worst thing that can happen is that things continue the way they are for the African-American community."

It surprises me that some people didn't want to give him a shot. The black community already knew what to expect from Hillary Clinton. Barack Obama did nothing that was specifically aimed at the black community, which disappointed many people. He did things that were specifically for the gay community, the banking community, and the auto industry.

The black community thought that because the country had elected a black president, he would make positive changes for his own people. Obama was supposed to be the great unifier, the bridge builder for this country. But black people alone did not elect Obama president. White people did, too.

A lot of Republicans voted for him in that first election. They gave him a chance. America gave him a chance. America proved that it is not the racist society that some portray it as. What's the proof? America elected a black man president.

But under Barack Obama, racial conditions worsened. Blacks were back rioting in the streets. If you criticized Obama and you were white, you were automatically deemed a racist. President Obama and the First Lady, Michelle Obama, played that card very well.

President Obama got a pass from the black community because the influencers and the trendsetters in the black community are the athletes and the entertainers, and they embraced him.

Because the athletes and entertainers embraced him, their fans embraced him as well. If anyone criticized him, an athlete or an entertainer stepped up to defend him, and the masses of fans followed along.

If you were black and had the audacity to criticize Obama, you were deemed a race traitor, a racist, a coon, an Uncle Tom, or a sellout. In the black community, there's a code: if there are blacks in public arenas, other blacks are not to criticize them in public. It would be almost like snitching to the police.

Since he stopped being president, Obama has not gone back and advocated for or been active in the black community, either. In the black community, he had assumed near messianic status upon being elected, but he became an unspoken disappointment to many.

I was at a meeting at the White House with black pastors in 2018. I said something that went viral, and it's my truth:

"Donald Trump is the most pro-black president in my lifetime. I've lived under twelve different presidential administrations. I was born under Eisenhower's administration; I lived through Eisenhower, Kennedy, Johnson, Nixon, Ford, Carter, Reagan, Bush, Clinton, Bush, Obama, and Trump. Twelve presidencies. He's been the most pro-black president in my lifetime.

When I use the word 'pro,' I'm using the word 'pro' in the sense of being proactive. He's the most proactive. All of the other presidents in my lifetime have been reactive toward blacks. President Trump has been proactive toward blacks."

I meant "reactive" in the sense that the major accomplishments of blacks in my lifetime have come as the result of social upheaval, disorder, outrage, and activity. The Civil Rights Act of the 1960s was signed into law by President Johnson because of the pressure brought upon him by the civil rights movement and by social upheaval in America. We were rioting in the streets. Dogs were set on people; black people were getting beat by police. The social climate produced the Voting Rights Act.

Actually, that bill was introduced in the fifties under Eisenhower. Johnson was one of the people who stonewalled it. But it was the result of Jim Crow laws and black unrest—civil unrest. There were other things, like affirmative action. But it seems like everything that was done for the black community was done as a reaction.

President Trump has been proactive. Prison reform is a proactive movement. It's something that was not the result of social upheaval or civil unrest. I'm on the president's prison reform board, and I went to the very first prison reform meeting. A number of governors were there from all over the country, along with people active in prison reform—those with prison ministries and those who had privatized prisons. No one advocated for prison reform in that meeting more strongly than Trump.

Trump would say, "Well, you know, they're not all bad guys. Even though they're in prison and did bad things, a lot of them have learned their lesson and paid their debt to society. They deserve another chance. What can we do to help them? What can we do to help curb recidivism?

Maybe I can talk to different companies about giving them jobs."

The 1994 crime bill under Bill Clinton disproportionately incarcerated African Americans. We were being locked up left and right for things that other races were not getting locked up for. That Clinton crime bill was horrible to the black community. A woman I knew was caught with an empty crack pipe; it was in someone else's car that she was driving. She got stopped for a broken taillight, the car was searched, and the pipe was found. She was sentenced to two years by a hanging judge. She had a baby daughter, only three weeks old, and she was separated from her daughter and sent to the penitentiary. The Clinton crime bill separated more black fathers from their homes, too, and destroyed the unity of more black families than this so-called border crisis ever will.

President Trump incorporated criminal justice reform along with prison reform. He did it simply because it was the right thing to do. The president passed opportunity zone legislation as a way to revitalize the black community, through incentivizing investors to invest in our distressed urban communities; the legislation created the largest public-private partnership for urban America in American history. It was ingenious that he signed this legislation into law, because now there's no need to go through Congress to get legislation passed to produce the money; the money comes from private investors.

Kareem Lanier and I produced a detailed plan as part of the Urban Revitalization Coalition we founded (more on that later), and we were able to put that plan into the president's hand and into the hand of Jared Kushner, the president's son-in-law and one of his chief advisors.

Jared, whom I had come to know during the campaign, is one of the most down-to-earth people I've ever met. As a matter of fact, all the Trumps are like that. First Lady Melania, Donald Trump Jr., Ivanka, Eric, Tiffany—and, by extension, Jared and the president's daughter-in-law, Lara. They are not prototypical billionaires' children, not high-minded or snooty at all. They're all friendly and grounded. I think that's a testament to Trump's personality. The president once told a group of us, "Listen. Other billionaires call me to ask my kids to counsel them."

His kids are not the kind of billionaire kids that you see in Hollywood, the ones who are or were drug addicts or dopers or stoners, the ones who get into trouble. Trump puts his kids to work. At the RNC, Don Jr. said something I found remarkable: "We're probably the only billionaire kids that know how to plaster, know how to hang drywall, know how to do electrical, know how to operate a backhoe."

Their father raised them up on construction sites and made learn how to do the work. He instilled a strong work ethic in them. Don Jr. said that his father would call him at five in the morning and ask him if he was at the office yet.

When I met Tiffany, I thought she was a secretary or an assistant, because she was very humble and friendly. When I met Jared, he approached me, introduced himself, and said, "My wife and I were watching TV one night and saw you on CNN. You absolutely kicked butt. My wife and I love you." We shook hands, and he gave me his phone number.

Jared is a genius—an unsung, unappreciated patriot with great political instincts and a heart for this country. If it had not been for Jared Kushner, the prison reform bill wouldn't have passed. There wouldn't have been any criminal justice reform. He contributed to the creation and passing of the opportunity zones initiative. He does not seek the limelight; he's not self-aggrandizing. He works tirelessly and has a great sense of dry humor. We bust each other's chops all the time.

He'll go to my wife and say things like, "I don't see how you put up with this guy."

Or I'll go to the White House, and he'll look at me and say, "Hey, who let you in here? Somebody call security."

The first time I met Ivanka was at Trump Tower, right after she had her last baby. I was on the twenty-fifth floor, standing at the elevator, and a lady was standing there.

She said hi. We both got on the elevator, and I realized it was Ivanka. "How are you doing?" I asked her. She was very friendly and polite, and we had a great conversation.

Melania is about the nicest person you'd ever want to meet. She has always been very friendly to me and my wife. She always asks me, "Where's your wife? How's your wife?"

If my wife is there, they segue to girl talk. She's a mother. I always ask her about her son, Barron. I've always been very sensitive to that. Barron is the same age as my granddaughter.

During the campaign, I asked her, "How's Barron taking this?"

She said, "Well, I try to keep him away from the television. I keep him away from the negativity." She covers him, as any mother would, and she protects him.

Lara Trump has become a very special friend of mine. She has great Southern charm and hospitality. During the campaign, Lara headed up the Women for Trump coalition.

She spoke at my church and did a great job. I've always told her, "You've got some preacher in you."

* * *

Being a business owner, pastor, and leader of people for more than twenty-five years gives me a degree of understanding about Trump that I think a lot of other people don't have.

It's a very different mindset when you're a leader and a boss. This president has never been someone else's employee. He's been a boss all his life. All good leaders have to have a certain degree of narcissism. They have to have a lot of self-confidence. They have to have a healthy dose of self-esteem. Trump had to have a certain degree of narcissism just to be able to enter this race in the first place. He's a master with the media; some of it is genuine, some of it is schtick, some of it is his persona. He has a self-deprecating sense of humor in private.

In fact, Trump is a very funny guy. Even if he wasn't the president, I would still love to hang out with him. He cracks me up just being himself sometimes.

And it may be one of the secrets of his marriage. I was with Trump and Melania on Election Night 2018. Trump turned to his wife and said, "You know, Melania, he said that he likes Michelle Obama better than he likes you." She laughed.

I said, "No, I didn't."

She said, "I know he's just kidding," and she laughed some more.

Another time, Trump showed me the Lincoln Bedroom. He said, "I had someone stay here, a friend of mine. The next morning, I asked him, 'How'd you sleep last night?'"

His guest said, "I slept well."

The president asked, "Did you like the bed?"

"Yeah, I liked the bed."

Trump delivered the punch line: "You know Lincoln's son died in that bed."

We were all laughing. Melania was cracking up. I noticed the way President Trump was looking at her. She laughed, but in that laugh was love, and in that love was a relationship.

I looked at her and said, "He cracks you up, doesn't he?"

"All the time."

I don't care what the media says. They've got a good marriage, and that's one of the keys to a good marriage—humor.

* * *

A lot of people might find this surprising, but in private, Trump is a very humble guy. He's even a little bit shy. However, he's very comfortable and outgoing in front of a crowd.

He had to make the difficult transition from being a public figure to being a public servant. It's a very big, very difficult step to take, no matter how easy one might make it look. That transition happens faster physically than mentally or emotionally.

Trump wasn't used to having to guard his words or reserve his opinion. He wasn't used to having every single word that he said microanalyzed and scrutinized, and then twisted and used against him. He was used to shooting from the hip whenever and however he chose. He wasn't used to having to answer to anyone about anything.

There has never been and there will never be another president like this one: a nonpolitician—a businessman, a boss—who became president. It's not like he was a businessman who ran for Congress, and then ran for Senate, and then was a vice president, and then became president. You're talking about a guy who went right from the private sector to the highest public office in the land. It was unprecedented.

He puts his game face on, and he keeps his game face on, and he wears it very well. If he's having a rough time or a difficult day, you'll never know it. He never lets anyone see him sweat.

But he had to make that transition. He went to bed a private citizen, and he woke up the leader of the free world.

I think he's handled that transition very well. He's done it while retaining his personality, his sense of humor. His persona. That's not an easy thing to do.

* * *

My second choice for president in 2016 would have been Mike Huckabee. I love Huckabee. I love his outspokenness. I ran into him one time in Fox's studio when we were both appearing on Sean Hannity's show.

I said, "Hey, Governor, how are you doing?"

He and I had become friends during the RNC. Huckabee plays bass guitar, and I wanted him to come out and play at my church during the RNC. He said of himself, "This white boy has got a lot of funk up in him." I thought that was very funny. He's not only a great guy and a good politician, but he's also a very strong Christian and a great representative of the Kingdom of God. Trump hadn't chosen a vice presidential candidate at the time I saw Huckabee at Fox, and I was hoping he would ask Huckabee to be his running mate. I told Huckabee I would put a word in for him, but before I could, Trump chose Mike Pence.

It was an outstanding choice that balanced the scale. Mike Pence is a great man, a godly man, a Christian man. His wife, Karen Pence, now the Second Lady, is great. His daughter is great. She bonded with my wife at an event he attended in my church. Pence appears in public as a very buttoned-up guy, but he's not. He has a great sense of humor. I like him a whole lot. And the president respects him very highly as a paragon of virtue.

It's my opinion that Omarosa doesn't care for Vice President Pence, however. I believe she doesn't trust him because she couldn't crack him. She couldn't get a good read on him. The vice president plays his cards very close to the vest. I've seen him at a number of events, and he's always been very friendly with me. He is the vice president of the United States, and he always goes out of his way to shake my hand.

Pence also knows how to dap pretty well. So does the president. We've got our own dap. He's a great balance for the president.

President Trump likes to surround himself with godly people. He likes godly influence. Jerry Falwell Jr. is a great friend of his. Jerry and his lovely wife, Becky, have become great friends of mine as well. Trump also has a very high regard for Franklin Graham and his daughter, Cissie, and they've also become friends of mine. He has a high regard for Paula White, not confusing her friendship with her calling. He reciprocates the friendship, while respecting her calling. I commend him for that.

As I've stated several times, when Donald Trump is in a room with preachers, he adopts the position of the lesser and sees the preachers to be in the position of the greater. He continually states that he believes preachers should have a greater voice in American policy.

When people question me about Trump's Christianity, I respond by saying that he believes all its major tenets—the foundational precepts and doctrines of Christianity. He believes in the existence of Jesus Christ, the Virgin Birth, and the vicarious sacrifice of Jesus Christ on the cross at Calvary. He believes that Jesus died for the sins of human-kind. He believes in the burial and resurrection and ascension of Jesus Christ into heaven, and he believes in Christ's second coming.

Someone asked him whether he ever asked God for forgiveness, and he replied that he tries not to have anything to ask forgiveness for. I think that was a smart answer, because if he had said yes, he would have been grilled about what he had asked forgiveness for.

Personally, I believe he has asked God for forgiveness many times. I believe that when he lays his head on his pillow, he continues to ask for guidance, like he asked the preachers to pray for him many years ago.

I always said that there was no way Trump could lose the 2016 election, because I never saw a candidate receive as much prayer on the campaign trail as he did.

There is a doctrine in Christianity known as sanctification. It is a person's individual walk with God, something totally between God and that person. The Bible says, "Man looks at the outer appearance; God looks at the heart." A person's individual walk with Christ is between that person and Jesus. It's not up to us to critique it. When the Lord says, "Judge not that you be not judged," He is not saying for us not to make decisions or evaluate people's behavior. He is saying that you can't evaluate their motives. You can't know a person's heart, so there's only a certain amount of judgment you can have.

Trump's not a theologian. He's not a Bible teacher. His working knowledge of the Bible seems limited. Some people who have gone to my church for twenty years still have a lot of struggles. I know preachers who preach the gospel every week and cheat on their wives, use drugs, or are closet alcoholics. We look at people who visibly practice Christianity, and we hold them up as paragons of virtue. Trump's walk with God is a personal matter between him and God.

President Trump embraces the Presbyterian faith. He says that he's a Presbyterian by persuasion. Presbyterians are evangelicals. There are different factions in Christianity, such as Calvinists and Arminians. Calvinists believe "once saved, always saved." That salvation is irrevocable. Arminians believe that you can forfeit your salvation. Calvinists believe that salvation is utterly up to God; Arminians stress the importance of free will in salvation. The Presbyterian Church is evangelical in persuasion, and evangelicals are, by and large, Calvinists. There's a faction of Pentecostals, and there are other Christian denominations that are Arminian.

I'm a Pentecostal. Pentecostals believe that salvation can be forfeited, that it can be gained and/or lost. Calvinists believe that it can't.

There are five basic principles of Calvinism that can be expressed in the acronym TULIP. The first, the "T," is total depravity of man—meaning that man in and of himself is totally depraved. Man has nothing in him that desires God, that reaches out to God, that seeks God. Any interaction between God and man is only by the overtures or the initiation of God. Man can't reach out to God; God has to reach down to man.

The next one, the "U," is unconditional election—meaning that God, according to His own decision, unconditionally selects some people to be saved and others to be damned. Anyone who is a believer or a Christian or saved or enjoys salvation has been selected by God for salvation. Anyone who is lost has been determined by God to be lost.

The next precept, the "L," is limited atonement, which means that Jesus's sacrifice on the cross was only for a select group, those who have been unconditionally elected to salvation. After that one comes the "I," irresistible grace—meaning that if God does select someone for salvation, there's nothing that person can do to resist it. You're either saved or you're damned. You're either lost or you're found.

The final one, "P," is eternal perseverance—or as we like to call it in Christian circles, "once saved, always saved." If God unconditionally selects you for salvation, there's nothing you can do to lose it.

Trump is a Calvinist, so evangelicals can support him without compromising their Christianity, based upon the fact that, if you're a Calvinist, either he is a Christian because God selected him or God didn't do it. It's not up to me; it's up to God, whomever He elects, or whomever He does not elect. That's why evangelicals can stand next to him: because you never know definitively whom God has selected.

Some giants in Christianity in the past several decades, great and notable men and women of God, have committed transgressions and fallen from the height of their platform. I don't want to name them, because a number of them are still alive. Everyone expected them to be great paragons of Christianity, but they had secret transgressions and secret sins that they were engaging in. It's up to God whether they were saved or not. God knew what they were doing when they were doing it, whether anyone else knew or not.

In the Bible, when Saul is transgressing, David says, "I won't touch the Lord's anointed." Also in the Bible is Cyrus, a non-Jewish, non-Israelite king, but God calls him His anointed servant. Why? Because He raised Cyrus up to treat His people with favor.

Trump is the most pro-Christian president I've ever seen in my lifetime. He's not ashamed or afraid to promote and defend Christianity—or Judaism, either. He has become a protector of the church, a protector of Christian values, and I don't think he's doing it just for the evangelical vote. He's become a protector of Israel as well. I believe that God called him and raised him up "for such a time as this."

In private conversation, Donald Trump has said to a room full of preachers, "Who better should speak to the problems and the ills of society than preachers?" He said, "Preachers are the ones that should address the negatives of society. Preachers are the ones that should speak against crime, and violence, and filth, and degradation, and sin."

He said, "It shouldn't be the politicians only that do this. It should be the preachers that set the moral temperature of America. Not politicians." I believe that God raised him up because under Obama, the church was getting a bad rap. I believe that Obama initially professed to be a Christian in order to get the Christian vote. The United Church of Christ, which he identifies with, lies beyond the pale of orthodoxy—in terms of the fundamental precepts of the church, it deviates from orthodoxy.

Obama was a member of that church under Pastor Jeremiah Wright, who was into black liberation theology. He sat under the pastor for twenty years. You can't tell me he sat under him for all that time and didn't imbibe some of that man's spirit and thought processes. Obama acted as if he was a Christian until he got reelected. After he was reelected, he began to be, to me, one of the most anti-Christian presidents America ever had. He began to denigrate Christians in public, and he began to somewhat ridicule and even denounce Christianity, because apparently he didn't value the Christian vote as much anymore. I don't understand how so many Christian black pastors could support him.

I was naive enough to automatically believe that all Christians are conservative. That all Christians are automatically pro-life. That we have certain moral standards and viewpoints regarding homosexuality, abortion, the right to life, and other issues. Obama began to position himself on the opposite side of those standards and viewpoints. But Donald Trump is pro-Christian. He's pro-Jewish. He publicly endorses Judeo-Christian values.

TEN

Nobody had a problem when, during the 2008 campaign, I allowed Barack Obama's supporters to come over to the church. He sent several high-profile actors from Hollywood, including Giancarlo Esposito and Hilary Swank with her then-husband, Chad Lowe. A number of politicians from all over the country would come to my church, and I would give them time in the pulpit to advocate for Obama. In fact, for decades, statewide and local politicians would come to my church, and I would always afford them time. No one ever complained about separation of church and state. No one ever said that I shouldn't allow in my pulpit judges and politicians who were running for office. I always had an open-door policy regarding candidates from both parties, who would solicit support from my members. But as soon as Donald Trump decided to run for president, everyone started screaming about separation of church and state.

They didn't actually mean separation of church and state; they meant separation of church and Trump—that I shouldn't allow Trump in, but I could allow Hillary Clinton or any of her representatives in. All this controversy began to take a toll. Church members began to leave, and I would get letters.

I asked one member why she was leaving. She looked at me and said, "Trump."

I didn't understand this. Number one, I would think that people would be open-minded enough to do as the Bible says, to "judge righteous judgment." Number two, they had me, somebody they know and claim to trust, telling them that the media's narrative was fake. It was disheartening to me that some chose to believe the media over their pastor, that some allowed CNN and MSNBC instead of me to pastor them. My integrity and credibility had never come into question before.

My wife and I have been noteworthily generous during the course of our ministry. We have many programs in our church. Through Operation Recovery we feed and clothe the homeless. We have given away food on a regular basis, to members and nonmembers alike. We have purchased homes for members to live in and have paid rent, mortgages, and utilities. We have bought cars for many people, and bought vans for our church to provide transportation for those who have none.

The members who left told me that they had prayed about it and God led them to leave. The Bible says that it is God who determines who is in authority over nations and countries. By that logic, it's God who set Trump as the president. If God knew, in His omniscience, that He was going to elevate Trump to the position of president of the United States, He wouldn't lead people to get offended and leave their church because of it.

A lot of people have been deceived by fake news. It irritates me that people would believe the media over their pastor. It reminds me of how in the Bible, Jesus's ministry attracts controversy and "many of his disciples went back, and walked no more with him."

An elder of my church turned into a Trump basher. He was outspoken about the Billy Bush tape and about the women who said they had been groped. He was a guy who sat in my office and received counseling from me because his wife discovered that he was going to strip clubs and soliciting strip dances, among other things. Rather than expose him, we covered him, counseled him, prayed for him, and ultimately restored him. His criticism of Trump was very hypocritical to me.

I commend the members who have stayed with me and stayed strong, even though they have had to undergo a lot of antagonism. At times, the Black Church can be very cruel and hypocritical. We are taught to love our neighbor. We are taught to be kind to one another. We're taught to judge not, that we not be judged. But the majority of the attacks on my church and its members came from other Christians—the churches and the pastors.

The people who boycotted our church, marching around outside, were other Christians. I used to tell them, "Why don't you go picket the abortion clinic? Why don't you protest against the dope house? Why don't you protest all of the things that you preach against? Why are you protesting against a church?"

It was very fake, very phony, and very disappointing.

The Black Church embarrassed itself by its conduct during the 2016 campaign. The Republican Party more closely reflects the principles and ideals of Christianity than the Democratic Party does, so I can't understand how the Black Church in general could be enamored and supportive of the Democratic Party, which espouses and promotes things that should be, or supposedly are, diametrically opposed to the principles and the precepts of Christianity. The Black Church denounced and criticized me more than they criticized Louis Farrakhan, who openly denounced and denigrated Christianity.

As I mentioned, our building is a multipurpose facility, with a banquet hall, a stellar award-winning gospel radio station, and more, and a number of the preachers pulled out because of my association with and support for Donald Trump.

In my opinion, a lot of black preachers are some of the biggest cowards in America. They're afraid. They trust in themselves and their congregations more than they trust in God. They look at members as offerings, and they're afraid to hurt their cash flow. They are afraid to take a stand for anything that is controversial, anything that goes against the grain. They've said this to me out of their mouths: "I like Trump, and I'm going to vote for him, but I can't let my congregation know."

People would ride by my house, stop in front, and point. My grandchildren got into conflicts in school. People would follow my wife home in her car, trying to intimidate her. They would confront my daughter on social media.

The house I was living in at that time had a lease option. When I negotiated the deal, the owner had run out of money because of the recession, and he wasn't able to finish building. I cut a deal that I'd move into the house with a lease option and then finish the house, which would serve as a parsonage. Whatever money was used to finish the house would apply toward the purchase price.

We leased the house for several years, finishing a major portion of it. When the lease expired, and it was time to exercise the purchase option, I decided not to. With the church exodus and the boycotts, purchasing the house at that time wouldn't have been prudent. When I told the owner I would not be purchasing the property, he got upset. I told him that times and circumstances had changed, and that my wife and I were going to scale down to a less expensive house.

He responded, "Well, just ask Donald Trump for the money. Trump will give it to you."

What the heck was he talking about? I was not going to ask Trump for money for anything.

After I moved, he filed a lawsuit trying to force us into buying the house. He used as "evidence" a copy of an *unsigned* purchase agreement between the two of us, and went straight to the media. Of course, because of my proximity to Trump, the bogus lawsuit gained national attention. I didn't comment on it publicly other than to say that it was a fake lawsuit. It eventually was determined that I owed the owner one month's lease payment. He declined to accept it. In fact, he apologized to me and said he had filed the suit only because he didn't want me to move, and that he talked to the media only because they called him incessantly when they saw the lawsuit in court dockets. We are still friends to this day.

As time went on, in spite of the controversy, I continued to hold my ground. I refused to be bullied or intimidated, refused to compromise my message. I refused to allow anybody to see me sweat. I wouldn't compromise my calling. In the pulpit, I continued to preach Jesus Christ and his crucifixion. I wasn't going to renounce my intent or principles. And I was sticking with my political candidate, because it's my right as an American citizen. I told my church members to vote for whomever they wanted. Not everybody who stayed believed in Trump or supported him for president, but they believed in me. I said, "If you want to vote for Hillary Clinton, you vote for her. If I want to vote for Donald Trump, I'll vote for him," and they respected that. We did not allow politics or the media to divide us, to affect the love we had for one another, or to negate all the time we had spent together as Christians.

It's very sad that we, as a people, aren't stronger-minded when it comes to the media. I can speak of my people because I'm one of my people. We overreact sometimes, without processing or filtering what we receive. Black voters were told that if Donald Trump became president, we would go back to being in chains, back to being slaves. We were told that we would be oppressed and persecuted. It was a very unpopular and very unusual choice for a black person to support Trump.

But the exact opposite of what people were saying would happen has happened. In my private conversations with Trump, he made promises to me on behalf of the black community. I believed then, as I believe now, that he would be very proactive regarding the black community, more so than prior presidents, and he has proven me to be a prophet in that regard.

* * *

As I've said, Trump campaigned incessantly and is the biggest workaholic I've ever known. He has boundless energy. Trump is twelve years older than I am, but you would think he was twelve years younger. Another thing I find impressive about him is that I've never seen him have a bad day or look tired. I've never seen him depressed or dejected, confused or uncertain. He always has a positive attitude whenever I see him—upbeat, outgoing, and gregarious.

During the campaign, he was doing three, four, and five stops a day. I couldn't hang with him. He would look just as fresh on the last stop as he did on the first stop. He was criticized, castigated, chastised, and condemned twenty-four hours a day, 168 hours a week, fifty-two weeks a year. And it seemed like it just rolled off his back. But I know he has feelings and thoughts, too. He has a wife and children. They're a great family. My wife and I have made it a point to pray for him on a regular basis, to pray that God gives him the wisdom, knowledge, ability, and temperament to lead this great nation—because if anybody needs prayer, he does. I don't know how he's able to stand up under all the attacks and still maintain his sense of optimism, remaining basically the same person that he's always been.

One of his last stops before Election Day was in Cleveland. Dave Bossie and Steve Bannon were riding on the plane with him. Dave called me from the plane and let me know that they were going to be touching down soon at the I-X Center in Cleveland. I was able to meet them in the back. Dan Scavino was there, too. As I mentioned, Steve Bannon and I got along great and became friends, despite the left's attempts to brand him a racist white nationalist. We had a horizontal relationship: eye to eye, man to man.

It was like that with all the guys. Trump surrounded himself with a unique, diverse crew of people, and that crew set out to make history. We were unlikely allies in some ways. But Trump didn't look for the intelligentsia or those in the realm of academia. He looked for those who he thought had a common vision, a common purpose, a common focus, and a common determination. He looked for those who possessed the courage to stand by their convictions—those with guts! I think that we did a very good job of it. I think we made a mark that cannot be erased.

Trump left it all on the court after that Billy Bush tape. He didn't hold anything back. He got up off the canvas and went on the offensive, like a boxer throwing combinations. He just swung away. Talk about resiliency; this guy came back and started kicking butt. We could see the momentum shifting. We could see the narrative changing. There began to be a very real concern that Donald Trump was going to do something impactful and historic, regardless of the media polls—the Twitter polls said something entirely different than the weighted polls did. Trump was putting thirty, forty, fifty thousand people in the stands, and the left was claiming that he was getting creamed in the polls.

We were seeing something that had never been seen before in the annals of United States political history.

In addition to his team, others in the media supported Trump, such as Niger Innis, who's the son of the great civil rights activist Roy Innis. The great Larry Elder was out there and outspoken. Alveda King and Paris Dennard were out there for him, battling in the media on the left and the right. We were taking hits and getting criticized and getting called every derogatory name imaginable, but we fought tooth and nail for Trump and nobody jumped ship, because we knew that the sacrifice we were making and the attacks that we were enduring would not be in vain if we were able to win. If we lost, well, we were gambling with house money. Nobody expected us to win anyway, except us. I do believe that if we had lost, we would have been able to go back to our black community and they would have received us back. Forgiveness is a trait that I'm proud to say that the black community possesses.

But I didn't think he was going to lose. I looked at Hillary and I looked at Trump, and I thought he was the better candidate.

I know what my contribution has been and still is. Blacks who support Trump have several things to point to now. We can point to criminal justice reform. We can point to black unemployment being at an all-time low. We can point to prison reform, to opportunity zones, to all President Trump's accomplishments. We didn't have anything to point to in 2016. We didn't have a track record to build upon. We didn't have a political record to reference. We didn't have any legislation that had been passed. We had to look forward in faith. It's a lot easier to point to what someone has done than it is to look forward to what you're hoping someone will do. We have been out there fighting on that political battlefield. None of the black Trump supporters I've mentioned are coons,

Uncle Toms, suck-ups, or sellouts. They were all very intelligent, articulate, introspective, accomplished people.

They have refused to allow themselves to be bullied. They haven't backed down, compromised, or become neutral. They have stayed their course. I'm proud of them.

I consider them family. I consider Lynne, Katrina, Diamond and Silk, Alveda King, and many others as my sisters. Mark Burns, Bruce LeVell, Larry Elder, Paris Dennard, and a host of others are my brothers.

Mark Burns and I were on the telephone once during a particularly grueling time. Mark had been under attack, and they had come at him pretty hard. He said to me, "They're calling me the number-one coon in America."

When he said that, I couldn't help but laugh. I laughed so hard that he started laughing, too.

I said, "No, they're calling me the number-one coon in America." We laughed so hard that tears came out of my eyes.

Mark Burns is young enough to be my son, and because I was the one who brought him into the campaign, he started calling me General Coon. Because we're both Army veterans, I called him Colonel Coon. We would do certain things to make light of a serious situation. If he called me on the phone, I'd answer: "Uncle Tom hotline. Can I help you?" Or: "General Coon here. Can I help you?"

If I would call him, he would say: "General?" And I'd say, "Colonel."

In fact, to this day, he and I still call each other General and Colonel. We do this to alleviate our shared pain over how people have treated us for advocating for a candidate who has promised to be beneficial for the African-American community. A candidate that we had spent a great deal of time with in conversation about how to best help the black community, knowing full well that we were not, are not, never have been, never will be anybody's Uncle Toms.

Whenever we would go on left-wing media networks, such as CNN and MSNBC, the deck would always be stacked against us. It would be one of us and three of them—one of us taking on a gang. We very rarely went one-on-one with anyone, unless it was the host of the show, and even then the host had the upper hand. The host would have the louder microphone and the ability to cut us off if we were making points.

When black Trump supporters went on, they would always have other blacks on to oppose us, as I mentioned previously. And the blacks would be the most disrespectful, insolent, insulting, and sarcastic toward us. Then they would get upset when I was disrespectful, insulting, insolent, and sarcastic toward them in return.

Believe it or not, I wouldn't trade that experience for all the tea in China. I'm glad that I experienced it. I think it made me a stronger person.

Oftentimes, when the media interviewed me, they would ask, "Well, you must be doing this for the money."

I would say, "What money? I haven't received a penny from Donald Trump."

People would say to me, "You're a sellout; you're only doing it for the money." I would respond, "I haven't gotten any money. Donald Trump hasn't given me a penny. I haven't received a penny from the campaign."

They would say, "You haven't?"

"No."

"Then you're stupid for not receiving money."

I'm still shaking my head over that—I'm either a hypocrite or a sellout if I do receive money, or I'm dumb and stupid if I don't receive money.

They put me between a rock and a hard place. But I know my motives have been pure.

During the campaign, I did an interview with a television station in Cleveland, and the reporter asked, "Are you doing this for money? Is Donald Trump paying you?"

"No, he's not."

"Well, are you seeking a job in the administration?"

I said, "No, I don't want a job."

She couldn't understand. "Well, what do you want?"

"I want the same thing that a person that is supporting Hillary Clinton and is not expecting a job or any money wants. I want my candidate to win, and I'm supporting my candidate."

I don't understand how anyone could see something wrong with that.

She asked me what I thought about people saying I was "selling out" my race.

I asked her, "If somebody asked you to sell out your race, how much would you ask for?"

She didn't want to answer. I pressed the question.

She finally said, "I don't have a price."

I said, "Well, what makes you think that I have one?"

She had no reply.

Although there was a black candidate for president in 2016, Ben Carson, blacks didn't support him. The black community by and large supported Hillary Clinton, a white woman who called blacks "super predators." Her husband, former president Bill Clinton, in conjunction with Joe Biden, who became Obama's vice president, passed a bill that decimated the black community.

As I've said, the Clinton crime bill disproportionately incarcerated African Americans. Larry Elder has stated that one of the greatest problems, if not *the* greatest problem, leading to the negative conditions in the black community is the absence of fathers. And some of the biggest factors contributing to the absence of fathers in the black community are welfare and incarceration. The crime bill put that three-strike rule in place. Bill Clinton's "crime bill" decimated the black community.

And there were also those subprime predatory-lending practices that began under the Clinton administration, when the banks were deregulated. The predatory-lending house of cards that collapsed under George W. Bush was built under Bill Clinton. Locking up black people, predatory lending to black people—these things started with the Clintons in control. Hillary Clinton's campaign and her side have demonstrated more systemic racism than any administration in recent history.

I'm grateful for the support that some of the black community is giving President Trump now. I'm very optimistic in believing we can receive 25 percent of the black vote in the 2020 election. I'm optimistic that with the accomplishments of this administration—criminal justice reform, prison reform, sentencing reform, low unemployment numbers for blacks, urban revitalization, and opportunity zones—the black community's standard of living can be elevated. I believe that the black community is smart enough to look at all the proactivity and think, "I need Trump to stay in office."

If he's not reelected president of the United States, it won't be for lack of trying.

ELEVEN

I n between the election and the inauguration, I told the president that I wanted to be a liaison between the White House and the African-American community, and he gave me the go-ahead. After he was elected, I heard from the critics and the detractors of the new administration, saying: "Well, where is his plan? Does he have a plan for black America?"

Roland Martin would ask: "Where is the plan? We want to know what his plan is for black people." In my mind I thought, *If this guy is the racist you claim him to be, why would you want him formulating a plan for our community?*

During the campaign, I had an idea for a racial summit. The year 2016 was the fiftieth anniversary of when Jim Brown had held the "Ali Summit" in Cleveland. A number of professional athletes—Bill Russell and Kareem Abdul-Jabbar, among others—attended. Mayor Carl Stokes was there. I had always envisioned trying to replicate that summit. I thought it would be good for America to bring together high-profile African Americans for a sit-down with the president, in light of the violence occurring in the black community and the racial tension remaining from the way the Democrats liberally "played the race card" during the campaign.

Jim Brown is a Cleveland icon. He was a black hero when I was growing up—a civil rights activist, very outspoken on matters of race and race relations. Not only is he the greatest football player who ever lived, but he is also the person who negotiated peace between the Crips and the Bloods in Los Angeles during the nineties when gangbanging was in its heyday. I was aware of his Amer-I-Can program, which offers life-skills training, vocational training, counseling, drug rehabilitation, and other services. I thought it could help offer solutions to the problems we were facing in the inner cities. I knew some people who knew Jim, and I set up a lunch with him and some of his friends and program coworkers to discuss possibly going to meet the president-elect in New York.

Because of the banging that his body took in his NFL days, Jim doesn't get around as fast as he used to. I think maybe he can run a forty-yard dash in only 4.7 seconds instead of 4.3. Eighty years old now, he is very intelligent, articulate, and thought-provoking—a well of wisdom and knowledge. He said, "In my day most, if not all, of the professional football players or the professional athletes were college graduates." Because they were college graduates, they had more of an expanded worldview. They had knowledge that athletes who are not college graduates don't have. I think it better qualified them or better equipped them to speak out on social issues.

I called Michael Cohen and told him I wanted to bring Jim Brown to Trump Tower and have a possible sit-down with the president. Cohen said, "No problem." He thought it was a great idea. He facilitated the meeting for December 2016. I told Bruce LeVell, the executive director of the National Diversity Coalition, to come, as well as my New York publicist, Adam Weiss, and his then partner, Matt Sheldon.

Belinda and I flew to New York. Jim Brown arrived with his lovely wife, Monique, as well as one of his friends and business partners, Bruce Zoldan of Phantom Fireworks, and former NFL linebacker Ray Lewis.

Omarosa met us outside. She took Jim Brown by the arm. Jim didn't know what she was doing, but he went along. She took his arm and walked through the door with him, and gave everybody the impression that she's the one who had brought him up there, even though she'd had absolutely nothing to do with the meeting. I thought, *She did it again.* Kellyanne Conway and Michael Cohen came into the meeting. Several people from the campaign staff were there as well. Trump listened as Jim told him about the problems of the gangs in the inner cities and about the Amer-I-Can program.

Trump said, "Some of the at-risk guys you're talking about are sharp guys. They're pretty sharp, huh? We've just got to refocus them. They could be an asset to the black communities. Listen, we have hundreds of millions of dollars in HUD [the U.S. Department of Housing and Urban Development]. We can talk to Ben Carson about possibly employing some of HUD's resources to help with the Amer-I-Can program, and to help with improving these conditions in the black community."

And then he said to Jim, "If HUD isn't able to contribute, I have my own money. I'll go in my pocket and write a check to help."

Everybody was shocked when he said that. I wasn't.

* * *

Jim Brown has always been outspoken about civil rights, always fighting for the black community. He has always promoted black empowerment, black advancement. He was one of the first blacks to be a successful businessman in a high-profile environment. He was one of the first blacks to own a record label. Earth, Wind & Fire began as one of his groups.

He was one of the first blacks to make movie production deals, obtaining financing to produce movies with black casts. He's been one of the most pro-black public figures in America, using his platform as an athlete and actor to advocate for social justice. He was and is a great black leader.

He went to the president-elect in Trump Tower to discuss how to advance the African-American community, and he was called a coon, a sellout, and an Uncle Tom by the "black left." He was called that by some people who were still a little wet behind the ears—snot-nosed kids who couldn't touch the hem of Jim Brown's garment, who weren't worthy to tie his shoes. I think the black community on the left, en masse, owes Jim Brown an apology. We're fortunate that he's still with us. In the Bible, Joseph tells the Israelites to take his bones with them when they departed from Egypt—meaning take the memory of his legacy and accomplishments with them when they went to their future destiny. I feel the same way about Jim Brown. The black community should not forget what he has accomplished on our behalf. He has done much more *off* the football field for blacks than he could ever have done *on* the football field. His career as a businessman, spokesperson, and social activist far outshines any of his sports accomplishments.

Jim and I made the rounds after that to CNN and Fox, and we went on Sean Hannity's show together.

* * *

I was honored to be on Trump's executive transition team. I considered it an honor that they thought that much about me to include me on it with a number of other political luminaries. It was a great experience working with great people. The team suggested candidates for posts within the administration, and I turned in the names of several people who were interviewed and considered.

Omarosa was thrilled to have been given a position within the administration doing African-American outreach. She had the biggest office in the Eisenhower Executive Office Building, almost an entire wing. She had a lobby area for her secretary and a large conference room. Trump took good care of her. The position was created especially for her, and she was probably one of the highest-paid members of the staff. I thought that she would do a great job regarding African-American engagement.

A little bit later on, late 2016, prior to the inauguration, I got a call from a preacher friend of mine, Luther McKinstry, out of Toledo, Ohio. He told me that he had been in touch with some former top gang members in Chicago who were now involved in community activism. They wanted to know if I could get them some type of help from the Trump administration.

Luther put me on the phone with a young man, T. Cooks. Cooks expressed his concern for Chicago. He let me know that it wasn't necessarily gangs that were causing all the violence, that young guys in cliques who were loosely connected were the main source of violence. He said that he had enough influence in the community to help stop the violence if he had more resources. I said, "I'll get in touch with the administration to help stop these black boys from killing each other."

I reached out to Jim Brown. Jim said, "Well, you have to know the terrain of Chicago. Chicago is very different." Jim put me in touch with one of the people in his Amer-I-Can program in Chicago. I was told, "Well, you can't just come to Chicago; you have to be invited in," and "You just don't understand."

I called Omarosa and said, "I talked to some guys in Chicago that are soliciting help from the president. They don't mind being public in their support of him, if and when he supports them in return." I didn't get a lot of traction out of it from her. She was busy trying to get support from the administration for the historically black colleges and universities (HBCUs).

She said, "Okay, I'll see what I can do," but I could tell that her interest in it wasn't high. Meanwhile, I continued having conversations with the guys in Chicago, letting them know that I would be doing what I could to reach out to the administration. We had several dialogues. I talked to Jim's people, and Jim's people weren't keen on T. Cooks. T. Cooks wasn't keen on Jim's people, either. Jim's guy was a little older; T. Cooks had more of a connection to the younger generation.

On January 31, 2017, eleven days after the inauguration, my wife and I were at home, preparing to go to church, when Omarosa called: "Can you guys be here at the White House tomorrow?"

"Tomorrow?"

"Yes, we're going to do something for Black History Month, and the president wants you there. Can you guys be here? You and your wife, and possibly pastor James Davis."

The next day was February 1, the first day of Black History Month. We immediately found a flight to D.C. We had to take a very early flight; the event was set for ten o'clock on the morning of February 1 in the West Wing of the White House. Ben Carson was there, too. Omarosa told me, "Listen. Don't mention anything about Chicago to the president, because I know if you do, he's going to pay attention to you."

I thought, *Wait a minute. I have my own relationship with him. I don't need anyone to try to navigate my relationship with the president, and I'm not going to let anybody control what comes out of my mouth.*

The president went around the room, allowing everyone to speak. When it was my turn, I told the president that there was a group of guys out of Chicago, top gang thugs in Chicago, who were not enamored with Barack Obama and the prior administration's treatment of them. I told him, "They like you, and they like what you're doing; they want to work with this administration about bringing their body count down," or words to that effect.

The media was waiting, and it seemed like that conversation overshadowed everything else that we were doing that day. "You said that you talked to some guys from Chicago," they said.

I responded, "I talked to them and told them that if they could help get that body count down, which they said they could do, this administration would be willing to help them and work with them about reducing the violence in Chicago."

I was at the airport to go home when T. Cooks called me. He said, "I was in the barbershop, and I couldn't believe when I heard that you'd said something about us. We're not gang thugs. We're men."

I said, "I didn't mean it derogatorily. That's just what came to mind." I added, "Hey, but I'm a man and you're a man. I don't have a problem walking it back." When some reporters contacted me, I told them that I had been at that event on two hours of sleep, that I had gotten up at four that morning to catch a flight to the White House, and that as a result, I had talked faster than I thought.

I said, "They weren't gang thugs. What they are are street activists, former gang bangers. They're street activists now."

The response from the masses was, "Oh, he lied. He said it was gang thugs, and then he walked it back; he lied."

No, I didn't lie. I had that conversation.

People in Chicago began to overreact because everybody was wondering to whom I talked. A lot of people said, "He made that up. That didn't happen." Then I gave the name of the person, T. Cooks. In fact, one of the Chicago newspapers did a feature story on him, and he was indeed who he'd said he was. He had the credentials that he'd said he had. He and I were trying to put together a summit to meet with them all. However, a faction said, "How dare you talk for us? You're not from Chicago. You haven't been here. You don't know what the hell you're talking about. Stay out of here."

I was making plans to go to Chicago and have a summit with these guys, so that we could listen to their concerns and then take those concerns, along with some of the activists, to D.C. to sit down with the president. A lot of people jumped on social media and bashed me, saying: "Don't come to Chicago. We don't want you here. You stay out of here." I'm not an activist in that respect; I pastor a church. When they started saying that, I said: "Well, forget it. I won't go then." I didn't go.

I canceled my trip to Chicago. Then a lot of the people who had said not to come started saying, "Well, why didn't you come? See? We knew you were faking it." I told myself, *I'm between a rock and a hard place with this. I'm trying to help my people, and a lot of them don't want the help.* But we wound up helping those who did want the help. We had a summit alright, in D.C. at the St. Regis Hotel. We had sponsors and bought plane tickets for a number of the people, T. Cooks and his associates.

We sat down and had a dialogue. I put them in the room with a lot of people who could help them: representatives from HUD and lending organizations, including Blue Sky Capital. I put them in communication with real estate developer Bill Pulte of PulteGroup, who was willing to come to Chicago and do some demolition work. I put them in the room

with the publisher of the *Washington Times*, and he bought them com-
puters and things like that. We had a great dialogue. But to this day I
still get criticism from people saying, "You lied about the gang thugs. It
didn't happen." But it did happen. What reason did I have to lie? Why
would I make up a lie about Chicago?

Then I had criticism on the other end: "You live in Cleveland. Stay
and try to solve the problems in Cleveland. Why are you trying to solve
the problems in Chicago?" My entire life, I've been a connector. I've been
a mediator. It's just a gift I've always had. When I was in the streets, I
always knew who had something, and I always knew who wanted that
something. I was a middleman between the consumer side and the distribution side for a lot of my life. And in my role as a pastor, I've had to
mediate a lot of conflicts—in homes, among families, in the community.

Our church has done a lot of community activism in Ohio. I've
always liked to help people with whatever resources or connections I
have. Chicago is still a work in progress. We're still having communication and dialogue with my contacts in Chicago. We're doing our best
to keep that on the president's radar screen. But you have to try to go
where you're wanted, and you can help only as much as those in need
of it will receive it. With Chicago being a Democratic stronghold—
or rather, in a Democratic stranglehold—I hope party politics aren't
allowed to continue to hurt the black community there. This president
wants to help, I want to help, and a number of others want to help. I
hope our black community doesn't allow politics to dictate and determine where the help comes from.

If you're starving to death and someone offers you something to eat,
you're not going to ask "What's your political party?" before you receive
the food. As long as we can get the assistance that is necessary for turn-
ing our community around, we should be appreciative of it. When I
spoke with President Trump about it, we discussed what can he do to
help Chicago and the other urban communities around the country. But
there's a process, and there's a lot of opposition. Some of the things that

Trump could do aren't done, simply because of the amount of opposition and the lack of cooperation.

Early in 2017, my friend and business partner Kareem Lanier, a Trump supporter during the campaign, approached me with a gentleman who was politically connected in Kenya. We had an idea for housing renovation in the urban communities that the Kenyans were interested in financing. Kareem is a very smart, aggressive, business-minded individual, a blunt talker. He's very well read. He graduated from one of the top private schools in Cleveland and attended the University of Dayton. He had been active for years in the mortgage and banking industry at this point.

He has a passion for the black community, and he's a member of the Christian community. His personality complements mine very much. He came to me with a proposal that had investors willing to buy houses in the inner-city communities. He proposed that, using money from investors, we buy houses from the city, renovate them, and then rent them out to members of the black community. Or, if possible, obtain a government subsidy for them. I mentioned it to Ben Carson at the Black History Month event, and he thought it was a great idea.

He said, "Listen. HUD does not want to be landlords, but we don't mind being tenants."

I mentioned to him that we were interested in doing that, looking to help improve the living conditions in the black community.

Kareem and I began to flesh this out. We began to contact people in different cities to get lists of available houses that the city owned, or that were part of the land bank and were relatively inexpensive. We were looking for houses, apartment buildings, and commercial buildings that we could renovate and revitalize, and in doing so, revitalize the entire community. We wanted swaths of houses—at least five hundred houses per city. As many as were available. It was a very aggressive plan.

As Kareem and I talked and strategized, we concluded that since the money would come from foreign investors, we had to ensure before securing funding that the business would be done right. After several conversations with the Kenyan investors and community leaders throughout America, we created the Urban Revitalization Coalition (URC) based on a very ambitious thirteen-point program model that included components related to transitional housing, banking, health and wellness centers, youth empowerment, retail, business, education, and criminal justice.

The plan took a lot of time and money to develop. The model was to be self-financed by the individual components, which meant that we had to acquire partners and sell them on our vision. We talked with a number of potential partners. Some showed genuine interest in revitalizing America's urban communities; others did not. Some agreed to participate; others did not. We were undeterred, because we knew the impact that our model could have upon the African-American community and the benefit it could be for the Trump administration.

The URC model combined the aforementioned components into a holistic city within a city that we would construct—a single multifaceted development. It would be the largest public-private partnership for urban communities in American history. After the model was created and we assembled the information in a presentable format, I secured a meeting with President Trump. I don't take my relationship with the president for granted, nor do I minimize the fact that I was able to gain an audience with him. I try not to abuse the privilege and waste his time on trivialities, but I knew that for our vision to be successful, I would need his approval. I also did not want to go public with a plan that he was unaware of.

Kareem and I sat down with the president in the Oval Office and outlined the entire plan. After perusing the contents of our brochure, he said, "This looks like great plan. What do you need from me?"

I said, "We need your blessing."

"You've already got that. You've always got that." Our desire was for it to become the largest public-private partnership for urban America in American history. The president said to us, "You know what? This is going to be the hardest thing you've ever done."

We wholeheartedly agreed. After discussing the business, we then laughed, joked, and made small talk for the remainder of time we had left, inquiring about each other's families and discussing the state of the nation. President Trump had not changed a bit since the day I met him, at least to me. He was the same guy, albeit with a great deal more responsibility than before. His parting words to me were, "Don't come back up here to see me again without bringing your wife." He and my wife have a very good relationship; they like and respect each other a lot. The president always marvels over the fact that she and I have been together for more than forty years. He always asks her how she could put up with me for that long a time. He also says, "You guys barely look forty years old." "Good hair dye," I always reply.

We hit the ground running. We began going to Washington, D.C., every week like traveling salesmen. We went to HUD. We went to the Treasury. We went to the Office of Public Liaison. We went to every one of the agencies we could go to. I already knew from the campaign a lot of people in key positions in a number of the agencies we went to. They were worker bees during the campaign but received key positions in different agencies after Trump was elected. That fact made it easier for us to go to them with our pitch.

We went around pitching our Urban Revitalization Coalition program model. We began lining up investors and partners through a lot of hard work. We went to Ja'Ron Smith, who worked in domestic policy and has since gone on to become a senior advisor to the president. Ja'Ron was instrumental in what we needed to do.

Ja'Ron is from Cleveland, like me—actually from the same neighborhood. I had met him at the Black History Month event at the White House in 2017. We had many of the same concerns for the African-American community. Kareem and I went to him with our plan, and he cooperated with us on it from day one. He gave us a lot of advice regarding what the administration could and could not do, as well as what required policy and what did not. He was very generous with his time from the beginning and still is now. Ja'Ron is a very detailed, meticulous guy who is a great help to this administration.

Jared Kushner heads up the White House Office of American Innovation. He had an open-door policy for us at the White House, as far as he had the time. He was very receptive to our pitch. We had a great deal of conversation regarding prison reform and criminal justice reform, which was and is a passion for him.

Ja'Ron was instrumental in writing the policy. He read over our material, and we talked with him on a regular basis. He said, "I have something that might help with what you guys are working on."

It was the Investing in Opportunity Act, which had been in the development stage for years. Ja'Ron was writing the policy for that. It was a perfect match for our thirteen-point program model that would serve as a plan for urban America. The Investing in Opportunity Act incentivized investors, by providing tax benefits, to invest their capital gains in communities around the country that were designated opportunity zones. It was an ingenious strategy. The president could motivate private investors to revitalize America's inner cities without the use of government funds, which prevented his critics from asking, "Where is the money going to come from?" The act would spur Americans to invest in America; it would motivate those who have taken resources out of the urban communities for so long to put resources back into them.

It also meant the president was able to get around being stonewalled by Congress, or by those who were antagonistic or in opposition to any of his policies. We knew the Democratic Party wouldn't want this to succeed, that Democrats wouldn't want him to "hit a home run" in the black community. Senator Tim Scott was one of the act's main architects. He was very driven to make this happen. After a lot of political maneuvering, the Investing in Opportunity Act was passed. It's what we're now relying on to finance the URC's program model.

The media started referring to our plan as the president's urban revitalization plan, which I was glad about. It gave our model a stronger base. We began to communicate with Jared and Ja'Ron more and more, presenting ideas to them to make sure they were feasible. Some of the ideas we took to them were accepted; others were rejected. They would say no, we can't do it that way, but we can do it this way. We were working together to improve the black community—to improve living conditions and revitalize the community.

Kareem and I were very persistent. We knocked on Jared's and Ja'Ron's doors and called them incessantly, as if they had nothing else to do. I know we got on their nerves sometimes, but they never let us know it. They were always very accommodating. Ja'Ron and Jared are both low-profile individuals who do not seek the limelight. They make a very good team. They're quiet, focused, and very determined, with no ulterior motives. They really just want to make America great again in whatever capacity they can. I don't go looking for the limelight, either, but I'm not afraid of it. And sometimes it seems to find me when I don't want to be found.

My purpose for the URC is threefold. First, to help the president keep his campaign promises to the urban community. Second, to help improve the living conditions of American citizens in the urban community, whoever is a part of it. Third, to get the Uncle Tom label off me and the racist label off the president. We had to do something to help erase those labels that the Democratic Party, and those who are antagonistic toward us, have tried to place on this presidency.

He'll keep his campaign promises to the black community. We'll help the urban communities, the distressed communities. We'll revitalize the African-American, and the Latino, and the Asian communities that are distressed. I think it's great and will be a very effective resource and tool. Our URC thirteen-point program model is bulletproof; it's criticism proof, because the only motive is to help urban communities.

I don't care what side of the political spectrum you're on; you should want to help urban communities. A number of community issues—violence, poverty, disrepair, and more—need to be addressed. Even though African Americans' unemployment numbers are down, things still need to be done to help the community as a whole. The URC and the Investing in Opportunity Act are going to go a long way toward helping to address these issues.

I began to outline the plan to different critics. Journalist Roland Martin was always asking, "Where's the plan?" Before I told him ours, I said to him, "First of all, why do you keep demanding a plan? Where's your plan? You keep asking me, 'Where's Trump's plan for black America?' Well, where's *your* plan for black America? Why don't you and all of your black intelligentsia and activist leaders put your brains together, pool your financial resources, and come up with a plan to revitalize black America? You keep criticizing Trump, calling him a racist. Why would you want a plan from a racist anyway?"

I called him and said, "We've got the plan."

"Where is the money going to come from?"

That was the question.

Initially we said that the model would be self-funded through partners. But when the opportunity zones were created and the Investing in Opportunity Act was passed, an entirely new source of financing was created that could potentially provide billions for us to achieve what we were endeavoring to achieve.

While the plan was still in the design stage, we called Omarosa, since she was in charge of black outreach. "Omarosa, we have this plan. You need to see it," I told her. "I want you to stand next to it and add your signature to it, give it your endorsement, because this is a very ambitious plan to revitalize the urban communities of America."

She did not show a lot of interest in it. When Kareem and I stopped by her office to give her a copy of our thirteen-point program model, she handed the brochure off to an intern, saying: "Here. Take this, read it, and write me some talking points about it." I never heard from her about it again.

I thought she would have been interested in it, that it was something she would have stood by. She had always been very accommodating to us in the past. She didn't give me any pushback, and she would always tell me, "If you need my help in getting some doors open, let me know." My guess is that she had enough on her plate. Our program model is pretty extensive and exhaustive.

* * *

During this time, I was invited to be on a number of boards, such as the prison reform board and the president's spiritual advisory board. I was honored to be included in the meetings. At the first prison reform meeting, no one advocated for the prisoners harder than President Trump. I was pleasantly surprised. Family members and friends of mine have been incarcerated; a ton of friends still are.

Trump said, "Just because they did something bad in their past doesn't mean they're bad people now. I think we should implement prison reform, so that they can reacclimate into society. I think a lot of them just need a second chance." I think that speaks volumes to the type of person he is.

Brooke Rollins had come onboard, too, and she was a great hire. She's not from Cleveland, but she happens to be a Cleveland Browns fan. She's a good person and very impressive. She stood up at the first prison reform meeting and said some very insightful things. It was a pleasant surprise to look up a month or two later and find that she had been offered a position with the White House Office of American Innovation, working directly with Jared Kushner. She was a very welcome addition to Jared's team—a big help to me and Kareem regarding our urban revitalization initiatives.

In some of our initial meetings with Jared on prison reform, Kareem and I were insistent that criminal justice reform be added. "Jared, you can't just do prison reform; there has to be criminal justice reform as well. Black people are being oversentenced. There has to be an undoing of that 1994 Clinton crime bill that disproportionately incarcerated African Americans."

Jared agreed: "You're right. But we have an attorney general [Jeff Sessions] that's still stuck in the eighties. We've got to get through to Sessions to do this criminal justice reform."

I went to Jeff Sessions at the end of one of the prison reform meetings. He was sitting in a chair, and I stood up over him. I was adamant.

I said, "Listen. You've got to implement criminal justice reform. We've got to overturn that Clinton crime bill." I put a document in his hand that contained policy for criminal justice reform that had been created for our URC program model.

He gave me a look that said, "Who do you think you're talking to?"

I said again, "You've got to overturn that 1994 Clinton crime bill."

Someone came over to talk to him, and it gave him an out. He got up to walk away, saying to me: "I'll look into it."

Yeah, right, I thought.

Once, when speaking with Jared about the problem of recidivism, Kareem said: "They're not returning to jail specifically because of the recommission of a crime as much as they are back in jail for probation violations. Technicalities. We need probation and parole reform as well."

Jared said, "I'll take that in consideration, but we have to take one step at a time." That's how he operates.

We had several meetings regarding prison reform and criminal justice reform. I also attended many meetings between the president and clergy.

I thank the president for thinking that I would bring anything of value to those meetings. He always came in with the attitude of, "What can I do to help you guys? What can I do to help the churches?"

Trump said in one of those meetings, "The Johnson Amendment muzzles preachers in their pulpit from commenting on political issues and being involved in politics, but who better to comment on social and moral issues than you guys? You should be the ones doing the commenting. The preachers should be the ones that spearhead efforts to improve the fiber of American society."

That's the Donald Trump I know and like. That's the Donald Trump I support. He wants to know, "What can I do to help you guys better serve your constituents?"

TWELVE

consider being a part of the president's spiritual advisory board a great honor. Paula White is its de facto head, a well-deserved position. As you know by now, I met Donald Trump through her. She has been a spiritual voice to him for over a decade, and took a very proactive position in the prison reform meetings as well. She and Trump have a unique relationship.

President Trump and I have different conversations than he has with her. Franklin Graham, Jerry Falwell Junior, and Pastor Robert Jeffress are spiritual advisors of his as well. Some have closer proximity to him than others, because there's a different level of friendship with all of us. The president shares some things with us that I don't think he has discussed with other people. The spiritual advisory board is about helping Trump navigate the spiritual terrain of the country, about advising him in matters pertaining to his office as president more than pertaining to his personal life. During our meetings, we discuss matters that we think to be of spiritual significance to this country.

The board has undergone some changes since it began during the campaign. I believe that some of the people on it got frustrated, because they thought it was going to put them in a position of reading the Bible to Trump, or just giving him biblical counsel, every other day. And there were people on it who I think should have never been on it. I never thought we needed the endorsement of any celebrity preachers. Those are the ones who don't want to do anything to affect or damage their profile or base.

When A. R. Bernard jumped ship, I was not surprised. He was never a Trump supporter but was allowed on the board probably because of his supposed reach into the African-American community. Behind the scenes, he affirmed his support of the president. But he would get in front of the cameras and say something else. He got his fifteen seconds of fame out of his defection. He had become part of the public conversation only because of Trump, and since he is no longer on Trump's clergy board, nobody is talking to him about politics, at least on national platforms. I think he missed a great opportunity to be of service to the country and to his constituents. They would have had representation in the White House.

When you're dealing with pastors, you're dealing with a room full of CEOs. It doesn't matter how large or how small someone's church is. That person is still the leader of that church. Because they're leaders of their churches, they have strong opinions—ideas that they think should be utilized—and everyone thinks that their idea is the most important idea. The president has to navigate and try to utilize them in order of importance.

The purpose of the spiritual advisory board is to have a voice regarding the spiritual direction that this administration is endeavoring to go in. I salute and applaud the president for even having the board. He's not the president only of the Christians. As much as I am totally biased toward Christianity—as much as I believe that Jesus is the only way, the only truth, the only light—there are a number of religions in America, and all of them claim to be the true religion. Trump has to give consideration to those as well. He has to have a Jewish component, an Islamic component, and other components of his spiritual advisory board. He has to try to represent a lot of different faiths that he does not necessarily subscribe to. In our country we have to have tolerance, and we have to have a certain degree of camaraderie with those of different faiths.

Maybe thirty to thirty-five people were at the first dinner for the board in the White House. The menu was great. Everyone had water to drink, but I looked over to the president's table and he was drinking Diet Coke. I asked a server, "Do you have any more Coca-Cola?" The server said yes and obliged. After the dinner was over, some preachers said to me, "How did you get a Coke?" I said, "I asked for it." It brought to my mind how the media made a ridiculous issue out of the president having two scoops of ice cream at an event while everyone else had only one. He had two scoops *because he asked for two scoops!* Anyone else could have done the same.

He called me up to stand next to him while he spoke, and he said complimentary things about me, which I appreciated. He always does that. Whenever he sees me in a crowd, he always acknowledges me with a wink or a finger point, or he summons me to the stage. It's very humbling.

I still believed the president would do great if we had a race summit. I still thought that a race summit would help clear up a lot of the misunderstandings that the left has been using to try to subvert American citizens with. A lot of those misunderstandings contribute to an untrue opinion of the president, even though people like Kanye West have come out and made statements in support of the president.

I mentioned the summit to the president, and he thought it was a good idea. I mentioned it to several other friends of the administration, and they thought it was a good idea, too. Jared thought it was a great idea but didn't think the timing was right.

I heard that General Kelly didn't like it. He didn't like the fact that I went to the president without checking with him first.

The race summit would definitely attract criticism. It has to be fair and balanced. It has to be constructive, not divisive. An exchange of ideas, not a sounding board or the grinding of axes. But some people in America don't want anything the president does to succeed, especially regarding matters of race. They don't want his policies regarding African Americans to be successful. They don't want him to improve living conditions in the African-American community. They don't want him to succeed regarding criminal justice reform and prison reform. They don't want to give him credit for low unemployment numbers or record stock market numbers. They don't want to give him credit for the economy or for our current military success regarding terrorism. They want to give the credit for those things to someone else.

During the 2016 campaign, President Obama said that you can't wave a magic wand and get manufacturing back. Well, Trump waved an invisible magic wand, and we got manufacturing back. If unemployment numbers during President Trump's time in office were astronomical rather than low, if jobs were absent rather than present, if the economy floundered rather than flourishing, Trump would get the blame. We have to give him the credit that he rightfully deserves.

I was on the original prison reform board; however, the meetings were expanded to include several black preachers from around the country, as well as several black personalities, like former baseball player and now minister Darryl Strawberry. Bob Johnson of BET fame participated, as did CNN commentator Van Jones. Behind the scenes, Van Jones is friendly toward the administration, but on CNN he feels pressured to bash President Trump.

It astonishes a lot of people that I'm as blunt in private as I am in public. I'm as outspoken and direct whether I'm sitting in a meeting with the president and his staff as I am on television or at a barbershop in the black community.

All who attended the prison reform meetings were experts in their fields, and those meetings were instrumental in making the First Step Act a success. The inclusion of the criminal justice element was an additional benefit; however, we hit a snag.

When it came time to take the legislation to the Senate floor for passage, Republican senator Mitch McConnell, the Senate majority leader, was reluctant. Van Jones told me on the phone, "Mitch McConnell is not taking this thing to the floor, and there's nothing we can do to get him to change his mind."

Whether McConnell and Senator Tom Cotton (R-AR) were trying to stonewall the bill or not, they were slowing it down. We were trying to get it passed before the end of the year.

Van told me, "You're the only one that I believe can get it done. You have to do it."

I talked with Jared. He said, "Yeah, Mitch has given us some pushback. He doesn't want to take it to the floor."

I said, "Wow."

That night while I was taking a shower, it hit me. I knew exactly what to do to get the bill across the finish line.

I called Kareem and said, "I'm going to play the race card." He laughed out loud.

I said, "The Democrats have been playing the race card since 2015; it's about time we played it back."

The next day, we called Senator Cotton's office and talked to their lawyers.

I wrote an opinion piece for the website Townhall. The headline was "Mitch McConnell: Get Up Off Your Butt and Pass the President's Prison Reform Bill."

I wrote, "If a tiny cabal of Republican Senators torpedoes this popular bill, it will be a slap in the face to President Trump's minority supporters, who already endure constant abuse from the left for our political and policy convictions."

I went on a couple of news shows on Fox as well, saying that the opposition "has racist overtones to it. Tom Cotton and Mitch McConnell will be the new Bull Connor and the new George Wallace if they stonewall this bill."

And I talked directly with Mitch McConnell: "Mitch, let me tell you something. If you don't take this vote to the floor, I'm going to come to Washington, D.C., with five hundred pissed-off black people, and we're going to tear some stuff up. We're going to come tear that Capitol up. Let me tell you something: White people protest nicely and politely, but when black people protest, we tear stuff up. If you don't do this, you're going to go down in history as a racist. We're trying to dispel that racist narrative that the Republican Party is being tagged with anyway. You've got to take it to the floor."

My wife heard me yelling on the phone. She said, "Who are you talking to like that?"

I said, "Mitch McConnell."

She said, "What? Get off that phone talking to him like that before the DOJ comes and kicks our door in!" I just laughed, but she didn't think it was funny. At all.

McConnell said, "I'll think about it."

Meanwhile, the clergy on the prison reform board conducted a pressure campaign of their own behind the scenes. I continued my public campaign, shocking host Harris Faulkner on Fox by insinuating that Cotton and McConnell would be branded as racists if they refused to take the vote to the floor.

After a few more days and a ton of phone calls and media interviews, Jared called me. "Mitch agreed to take it to the floor," he said. "I don't know what you said or what you did, but Mitch McConnell agreed to take it to the floor."

On C-SPAN, I watched the legislation pass while on the phone with Jared. We watched it together. When it passed, I congratulated Jared, because it would not have happened if it had not been for him. Jared deserves a round of applause. It won't show up in the history books. It won't be common knowledge. He might never get the credit that he deserves, but he is the one who made it happen. I think what he'll get is the inner satisfaction that comes with a job well done. Jared Kushner laid his soul on the line for the First Step Act. Job well done.

I give credit to each and every person who was a part of the effort. A lot of blacks participated in it, as well as a lot of whites. It was a bipartisan effort, Democrats and Republicans. It showed what we could do if we all worked together. After the act was passed, the White House had a meeting with black pastors whose churches had prison outreach programs. The meeting made television news.

Cameras were allowed in. This was an opportunity for us to discuss prison reform, an opportunity for these pastors to make the president aware of any initiatives they had. The president came into the room and greeted everyone. All present were afforded the opportunity to introduce themselves and share what was in their heart. Each one of them was extremely complimentary of the president. People were saying things to him that I don't even say. "Oh, Mr. President, you have the ear of God. God is talking to you." "Mr. President, I wish you would come to my church." "Mr. President, I'm glad to be here. I've been wanting to come up here for a long time."

I sat there while a pastor I'd known for twenty-five years told the president how glad he was to be there, and that he had been wanting to connect with the president for a long time but didn't know anyone who could connect them. I thought, *How can you say that you didn't know anybody who could connect you to Trump? I invited you to Trump Tower to meet him in 2015. Every black preacher in America knows that I have a relationship with the president.* I just shook my head.

Another preacher said, "Well, Mr. President, you have a relationship with Pastor Darrell Scott, and we want that same type of relationship."

The president looked unfazed. "Darrell earned that," he said. "We've been through a lot together."

Some of these pastors had criticized me for having this relationship, had castigated me for endorsing and supporting Trump, and now they wanted a relationship with him. If I had invited them to the White House, they would not have come. Paula White invited them, and they came.

Then one of them said, "Well, we need to have our own board. We need to meet more often. We need to select someone in this room to be our leader and our representative. We want to nominate Pastor John Gray for that position."

I was amazed at the privilege they felt. It was amusing to me. I have a relationship with the president, and I'm not threatened by anybody else. If anybody else has a relationship with him, that's their relationship. I have my own. I was sitting right there, and everyone knew that the president and I were friends and that he allowed me to be an advisor to him, and they wanted to nominate someone else as their leader. I thought it was funny.

After they flattered the president for more than an hour, he had to leave. More than twenty pastors were in the room, and with each taking at least three minutes to speak, an hour went by quickly. When President Trump rose to leave, he looked at me and said, "Darrell, you want to come back here with me?"

I went out the back with him to the Oval Office.

This was right around the time when Michael Cohen had begun to flip, and when we were alone in the Oval Office, the president said to me about Cohen, "Can you believe this guy?"

He knew how close Cohen and I were, but he didn't try to hold me accountable for Cohen's actions.

I said, "To be honest, I saw it coming. He had begun to be very negative."

The president said, "This guy is supposed to be my lawyer. He's supposed to be my lawyer, and this is the way he treats his clients? Wow."

I shook my head and said, "I think he began to sour because he wanted you to bring him to the White House and give him a position."

The president said, "Can you imagine if I had given him a job? Can you imagine if I'd have brought him up here?"

"You made the right decision," I responded. "For whatever reason, you didn't bring him up here. You had your reasons, and the decision not to give him a position turned out to be the right one."

"Whew," he said. "I dodged a bullet with that."

He didn't bash Michael Cohen to me, didn't say one bad thing about him other than to express his disappointment in him. I found that remarkable; I can't say that I would have done the same if I were him.

I went back into the preachers' meeting. They were still there dialoguing. Some of them asked me, "What did you go out back and talk to the president about?"

"I can't share what we talked about," I said. Then I told them, "You guys missed a golden opportunity. You had an open-windows moment."

"What do you mean?" they asked.

"You were in the room with the president of the United States," I said. "Cameras from every major news organization in America were in the room. The president went around the room and gave everybody an opportunity to speak, and you guys spent the time flattering and complimenting him. With those cameras on, you could have asked him for anything that you wanted, and he couldn't have refused you."

I continued, "If that had been me, I would have stood up and said, 'Mr. President, I'm Pastor John Doe from such-and-such church, and we have a multimillion-dollar community outreach. We need to learn how to secure government funding to help the homeless,' or 'Mr. President, I'm Pastor Somebody from Somewhere Church, and we need this and so such so we can do this and that.' He wouldn't have said no. He couldn't have said no. The lights and cameras were on, and you guys got caught up in the hype and forgot all about anything that you were doing, and you missed your moment. You're not going to get this moment back."

Some of them had tremendous prison ministries, crisis-assistance ministries, or outreach programs for the homeless, and they could have been much more effective with additional resources. God put them in the room with the president of the United States, and they got so overwhelmed at being in the White House with the cameras on that they failed to mention their missions. They didn't take advantage of that opportunity.

I told the people in the room what I mentioned earlier in the book, about how Donald Trump is the most pro-black president in my lifetime. The statement made national headlines.

The preachers all looked shocked. Nobody agreed, but nobody disagreed. My statement overwhelmed the entire meeting. I was vilified, criticized, and derided. I didn't care. I said what I meant, and I meant what I said. I wasn't going to walk it back.

All the preachers were called Uncle Toms, coons, and sellouts for attending the meeting. I watched John Gray on Don Lemon's show and saw Lemon intimidate him. Gray found himself on the defensive end: "Oh no, the only reason I went up there was because of this or that. I didn't know the cameras were going to be on." When Lemon brought up the part about me saying Trump was the most pro-black president, Pastor Gray said, "Well, I didn't say that."

I understand sometimes that discretion is the better part of valor. But when you're in the public eye and you call yourself a leader of people, you can't be fearful. You have to be courageous. People want courage in their leaders. They want fearlessness, and they don't want people who are hypocritical and deceptive. You can't criticize a guy in public and compliment that same guy in private. If I'm going to bash someone in public, I'm bashing them in private as well, and that's the way it is.

After the meeting was over, I said to certain people, "Don't bring those guys back up here anymore. I don't like secret supporters." You don't have to hide. You don't have to sneak. You don't have to pretend. Be just as brave in private as you are in public, and be just as brave in public as you are in private. Somebody criticizing you on social media is no attack. You can control that. All you have to do is not look at it. If you go out into the real streets of America, in the nitty-gritty of the black community—the streets of Chicago, Cleveland, St. Louis, and New York City—and ask the people struggling to survive if someone's making negative comments about them on social media is an attack or not. That's no attack.

I don't feel that kind of pressure, as I said earlier. Pressure is felt by people who are afraid to walk down the street because they might get shot and killed. Pressure is felt by people who are being oppressed in third-world countries. Pressure is felt by an unwed mother trying to decide whether to have an abortion or not. That's pressure. Somebody talking about you on social media because you sat down with the president? That's not pressure.

I feel like, for whatever reason, in His divine omniscience God has given me a door into the White House. God has allowed me to come up to the White House to talk to the most powerful man on the face of planet Earth regarding the direction of this great country. It's a privilege that I don't take lightly, and I will not allow people to cause me to despise that privilege. I'm going to make the most of this opportunity that God has given me to help my community and to serve this country.

THIRTEEN

A fter church one Sunday in 2017, the former mayor of Chardon, Ohio, approached me about running for Congress in my district, the 14th Congressional District. I was flattered and humbled by the request. Here I was, a guy from the streets of Cleveland being approached about running for Congress. I immediately declined: "No, no, I don't want to run for Congress. Thank you for asking, but no thanks."

However, members of the Republican Party were pretty insistent. They hadn't asked me to run on a whim. These were seasoned politicians, very active in the Republican Party. They really thought that I could win. They were dissatisfied with the incumbent congressman, David Joyce, who had made some negative statements about the president.

They said, "Don't make a decision, but think about it."

I weighed the pros and the cons. I was going on sixty years old and had been self-employed for years. I was set in my habits and patterns. I don't have to punch anybody's time clock except my own. I like having the freedom to spend time with my family. I enjoy the thrill of preaching. There's nothing better on the planet than that. I enjoy pastoring my church.

While I was still deliberating, I spoke at a Lincoln Day event, and I received very positive feedback. The 14th Congressional District is heavily pro-Trump, and they all knew and recognized me through my association with the president and as a native of Northeast Ohio. I wasn't concerned about opposition research. Every negative thing that could be said about me had already been said. My life and past were a matter of public record. I was just concerned that I wouldn't have the drive and the motivation to run for Congress. I was introduced to a potential campaign manager who was very knowledgeable and very capable of running a campaign.

I began to get phone calls. One lady tried to talk me out of it. She said, "Don't allow different people who are dissatisfied with Dave Joyce to get you caught up in their game."

Others said, "Why don't you run against Marcia Fudge?" Marcia was the successor to Stephanie Tubbs Jones, who was an iconic Northeast Ohio representative—and a very good friend of mine.

I thought, *Why would you tell me to run against Marcia Fudge? Marcia Fudge is black. Why didn't you suggest that I run against a white candidate somewhere else?* If I would have run against Marcia in her district, she would have annihilated me. She's a Democrat and the former head of the Congressional Black Caucus. I wasn't foolish enough to entertain the notion that I would have had a snowball's chance in hell of defeating her.

One thing people have to understand is the fact that our blackness still connects us. We're also both Clevelanders, and we can get together and discuss things that are beneficial for our community without being political about it. In fact, we've promised each other to work together to enhance our community. We have to have bipartisan efforts if we're going to make America great and make our respective communities successful.

I began to entertain the notion of running for Congress against Dave Joyce. One day I felt like doing it; the next day I didn't. I reached out to Corey Lewandowski. I reached out to Jane Timken, who was the head of the Ohio Republican Party.

I knew that it would put them in a difficult position, because they had an incumbent in office, and the party usually doesn't side against an incumbent. Out of respect, I contacted Bob Paduchik, who was cochairman of the Republican National Committee at that time.

"You don't have to ask my permission," Bob said.

I said, "I know, but out of respect, I'll notify you."

He said, "Wow, that's old school." Bob and I have become good friends since then.

I called Jane Timken to let her know that I was considering running, but that I wasn't doing it to offend anybody. Jane became a good friend as well. I consider Jane and Bob both very good friends. It's always pleasant when I see them. They're both great people, great Americans.

When I talked with Corey, he didn't try to talk me out of it, and he didn't try to talk me into it. He just asked me, "Why would you want to mess your life up like that?"

He didn't say "mess," he said "F" your life up like that.

He said, "You've got a good life. Why would you do this to yourself?"

"I don't know," I said. "Maybe the same reason that the president did it to himself."

He said, "Listen, you know me. If you're in, I'm on your side."

I reached out to some other people. I even made Vice President Pence aware of it. I ran into him at the White House one day and told him I was thinking about running. I didn't solicit anyone's support or advice, but I did solicit people's opinions, and I wanted them to give it to me straight.

One day, on my way to Washington, D.C., I was on the people mover with Kareem in Reagan National Airport, and a guy came alongside me and touched my arm. "Pastor Scott? Aren't you Pastor Scott?" I thought he had recognized me from the campaign or television, which happens all the time.

I was nice. "Hello, how are you doing? It's nice to meet you."

He said, "I'm Dave Joyce." My whole countenance changed. I immediately went on the offensive.

I said, "Dave Joyce? You're the guy that I'm thinking about running after to get your job."

He said, "Yeah."

"We've got to talk," I said. I got off the people mover.

"You've been out here dogging the president," I told him. "What's the matter with you?"

"No, I haven't been dogging the president," he replied.

"Yes you have. You made some statements."

He clarified the statements to me. He and I talked for a while as we walked through the airport, and I liked the guy. We looked each other in the eyes, talked, and shook hands. We promised that we would talk again. It was at that moment I told myself I wasn't going to run.

I had seen a genuineness and a sincerity in his eyes. After we parted from Dave, I said to Kareem, "I like that guy. I like him." He has the potential to be a great congressman.

My wife had never wanted me to run in the first place. "Haven't you done enough already?" she said.

As I've already mentioned, my wife is fearless, courageous, and outspoken. She's an excellent preacher, teacher, philosopher, and counselor. She's bold and assertive, but also calm, peaceful, and stable. She likes tranquility in her life.

She didn't ask for the constant criticism, harassment, and controversy. I took her on that journey with me. She was in agreement with a lot of the decisions that I made, and there were other decisions she was reluctant about. She has always supported me 100 percent, but you can support somebody without being in total agreement.

Sometimes she would just ask me, "Why? Why do you have to be the one to say something? Why do you have to be the one who stands up?"

I don't know why. It's in my DNA.

She said, "You don't have to fight every battle." She was not interested in a congressional run.

"Don't we have enough on our plate?" she said. "Aren't we fighting enough battles as it is? We've lost members of our church. We're still being boycotted, lied about, criticized, and attacked on a regular basis. We're trying to hold things together. We're still in the midst of a storm. This storm isn't over. Why are you trying to find another storm to get into?"

I didn't have an answer. Maybe I'm just a glutton for punishment.

She told me that she had prayed, and that the Lord hadn't given her a release regarding my potential run for Congress. My wife prays about everything. She won't go outside without praying.

Every time we get in the car to go somewhere, she prays as we leave that the house and our travel will be safe. Every time we get on an airplane, she lays her hand on that plane before we board, as we get to the door, and she says a prayer that the plane will go safely into the air and safely down at our destination.

She's my spiritual component. I shudder to think where I would be without her. If I had decided to run for Congress, she would have been there. She would have stumped on my behalf. But I would not run if she were not in agreement and had a release from God to do it.

My wife is a people magnet. She oozes charisma. In the first church we went to, when the pastor was done preaching, half of the people in the church would surround my wife. She's just magnetic like that.

I'd tell people, "You got the wrong candidate. She's the one who should run."

At one Lincoln Day event, I spoke for a little over half an hour. Poured out my guts. I got a good round of applause. My wife came behind me and spoke for five minutes and brought the house down. After it was over, everybody surrounded her. One or two people shook my hand, but the crowd was around her. That happens all the time.

We had the Values and Vision Conference, when then-candidate Trump came to our church and my wife prayed on him at the conclusion. A video of it went viral on the internet with the headline "This is the prayer that won Trump the election." She's just like that. When my wife speaks, she touches your heart. People who can touch your heart connect with you a whole lot better than people who can touch your head. I think she would have been a much better congressperson than me.

I know my liabilities, limitations, weaknesses, and flaws. I don't, as the Bible says, think higher of myself than I should.

I decided not to run, and Dave Joyce and I became friends after that. He won his election. His wife was fantastic as well. He and I have vowed to work together. He has told me that he will do anything he can to help our urban revitalization efforts, that I should feel free to call on him anytime. I've called on him on a couple of different occasions, and he has responded and been a help to me, and I appreciate him.

My congressional run ended before it even began. Thank God for that.

My wife was pleased that I wasn't going to run. However, I was still going to continue to be active with this administration. One thing that Kareem, Belinda, and I have impressed upon the president is the fact that the needs of the black community must be addressed. I don't think that a lot of the black members of the Republican Party can properly communicate the needs of the community. I know elected officials who say, "Well, I was born in the hood; I was raised in the hood," or "I was born in the inner city; I was raised in the inner city."

However, it's one thing to be *in* the hood; it's another thing to be *of* the hood. Some people lived there but weren't a part of that street life. Because they lived there, the people in the hood knew them and would give them a pass. But these guys went to school and graduated, then went to college, then became lawyers or professionals, and finally became elected officials. They were not a part of the hood culture. They might have dabbled in drugs—maybe smoked some weed—in their past, but they weren't out there selling and they weren't gangbanging. They weren't robbing, shooting, and/or killing, or doing any of the other things that the underbelly of the inner city participated in.

Unfortunately, I was part of the underbelly. I'm just a person who escaped. God laid His hand on me to get me out of it.

I believe that a number of the issues of the black community are not properly articulated by and to the Republican Party. It's not because Republicans are unmindful. We want to revitalize the people in the community just as much as we want to revitalize the physical structures of the community. We want to provide new and better housing, but we want to help prepare the residents to be homeowners. We want to support new businesses, but we want to prepare the residents of the communities to be business owners, to be entrepreneurs. We want to talk with them about community banking. And we have 100 percent buy-in, 100 percent cooperation, from the Trump administration.

Leading into the midterm elections in 2018, the president came to Cleveland for an event, and I had the privilege of opening the event with a prayer. The president was in a section in the back, and people would go back to shake his hand and take a picture with him. Kareem and I made it a point to be the last ones in line, because the one who is last in line gets to spend the most time with the president.

The president said to me, "I was meaning to call you, because I'm having an Election Night party at the White House tomorrow, and I want you and your wife to come."

I looked over and asked, "Can Kareem come?"

"Well, it's pretty full right now," he said. "But you know what? I'm the president. Yes, he can come."

We went there the next night to watch the election. Jared came and introduced his parents to us. I said to them, "It's a pleasure to meet you, Mr. and Mrs. Kushner, but you guys did a horrible job raising this guy." We all laughed. Jared laughed it off. Also among those in attendance were General Kelly, Candace Owens, Paula White and her husband, and Sheldon Adelson and his wife, Miriam. Miriam is fantastic and would receive the Presidential Medal of Freedom shortly after that night. Some of my favorite people on the planet, Ike and Laurie Perlmutter, were also there.

We were in the East Wing. The president immediately made me a part of his entourage. My wife and Kareem joined us. The president said, "I'm going to go over here to where the killers are."

There was a lot of power at that table. The president sat there telling jokes and busting chops, shaking hands with everybody and being the outgoing, hospitable guy that he is. This was the event I mentioned earlier, with the elegant buffet on one side and burgers, fries, and pizza on the other. Trump ate from the burger side.

Ben Carson came in, along with his wife, Candy. She and my wife sat together. They're very good friends. Franklin Graham came in, and my wife and he sat and talked as well.

When the president sat down to watch the election proceedings, he sat right next to our table. Dan Gilbert, owner of the Cleveland Cavaliers, came in. I'm a Dan Gilbert fan. I think he's the best owner that the Cavaliers have ever had, and one of the best things that's ever happened to the city of Cleveland. He's very active in Detroit as well. He and I have a lot of the same opinions regarding the Cavs, LeBron James, the state of the team, the future of the team, the history of the team, whatever. Everyone was having a nice time, but most people were reserved. At our table, on the other hand, we were wilding out—laughing loudly, telling jokes. My wife had to tell me several times to quiet down.

As the president watched the election returns, everyone watched the returns and watched him, too. When the Republican Party retained the Senate, he was very pleased. He said, "Well, I won one and I lost one." He was very upbeat.

Jared introduced me to the new staff lawyer and said, "Well, the Democrats have the House. We can prepare for a whole lot of investigations and litigations." It turned out to be a prophetic statement, because it's been nothing but that ever since. Ever since the Democrats claimed the House, they've done nothing but hold sham "investigations." We knew that they would come after Trump with both guns blazing, and that's exactly what they have done.

Nobody I talked with except Omarosa had any fear of being convicted, because we knew that it was all a sham. We knew that the whole Mueller investigation was a sham. We knew there was no Russian collusion. The Mueller investigation turned out to be the biggest dud in history.

Over the years, I've experienced many disappointments with people I thought were trustworthy. I had a very heated conversation with Anthony Scaramucci on the telephone recently regarding the president. He's become, for lack of a better word, an adversary. He's turned on the administration. He turned on President Trump. When I met Mooch during the campaign, he did not have the degree of access to the president that people thought he had. He wasn't in the inner circle like that. I didn't see him out on the campaign field much. The only time I would run into him was at Trump Tower. He was working in the war room, and this was very, very much later in the campaign. I didn't start seeing Scaramucci until almost election time, because he came on late. He wasn't part of the inner circle like so many people think. I was there. I know.

FOURTEEN

The purpose of the Urban Revitalization Coalition is to help the urban communities. Urban America is not comprised exclusively of black people. There are blacks, browns, and Asians as well. Additionally, the URC aims to assist the president in keeping his campaign promises to the black community. In one of his many campaign speeches, the president stated that he wanted to bring total revitalization to America's urban communities.

I do understand that revitalization can't happen only from the outside in; it also has to be from the inside out. If you put one bad apple into a barrel of good apples, all the good apples won't make the bad apple good, but that one bad apple can make all the good apples bad. Kareem and I realized that it would take more than just housing renovation and retail centers to revitalize America's urban communities. We're planning to construct youth empowerment centers that will have recording studios, computer labs, and a sports component in order to promote creativity and athleticism among our youth.

The plan includes components geared specifically toward the black community, and it's very innovative, comprehensive, and aggressive.

The passage of the opportunity zone legislation was perfect, because it allows anyone—not just those involved with the URC, but anyone who has a desire to revitalize urban America—to participate. It provides a means and a mechanism for people to acquire financing for their projects. In fact, there are a lot of people who have capital gains taxes, but they don't know where to deploy them; they don't have the projects. Our urban revitalization plan can marry the project with the money. I think it's a great benefit.

When the opportunity zone legislation was being fleshed out, Kareem and I embarked upon tours of urban communities so we could interact with the residents. We met with community leaders, pastors, council members, and community activists first, in order to explain some of the intricacies and nuances of the opportunity zones. After those initial meetings, we went back to meet with the general population—residents of the community who were interested in our message and desired change in their neighborhoods.

One event in Tallahassee, Florida, was particularly successful, with eight hundred to nine hundred community members in attendance. From there we went to Jackson, Mississippi, and Atlanta. Many people recognized me from my relationship with President Trump and, as remarkable as it may seem, we did not get much pushback. Some people came out of curiosity, but no one came with a hostile attitude. One lady stood up in one of the meetings and said, "Well, we were disappointed by the prior administration. They made us a lot of promises and then didn't do anything. We were disappointed. If we give you a chance, can you promise not to disappoint us as well?"

Kareem replied, "Listen, don't give us a chance."

The lady was surprised.

"We're not going to be held responsible for the lack of contributions of the last administration," Kareem said. "You're not going to hold us responsible for Obama's lack of performance." With the opportunity zones, the onus is on the communities to take advantage of the opportunities provided.

At one meeting I stood up and said, "When Donald Trump began to run for president, nobody gave him a snowball's chance in hell of winning. He won. What do you want us to do? He's not giving it back, and they're not taking it from him, as much as they would like to. Trump won; deal with it. We need to go forward and see how we can work together to better America."

We met with several influential investors and developers who are now on board with us. We're all excited about what the future holds. I find it refreshing that many whites are passionate about urban revitalization, that they want to correct social and economic disparities and atone for past inequities, and have committed to investing in America's urban communities.

We went to Kentucky at the request of then-governor Matt Bevin. After touring a facility for rehabilitating drug and alcohol users, we had a town hall meeting. There we met Evander Holyfield, who has since become a part of our urban revitalization efforts.

Kareem and I brought an entire team with us: our banking partner, our solar energy partner, our housing partner. Some Black Lives Matter activists in attendance gave us some pushback. I said to one of them, "What part of what we're presenting to you do you not want? Which of these guys do you want to leave this stage? The banking guy? The health-and-wellness guy? The housing guy? The retail or business guy? Tell me who you don't want here. Because we're here trying to help improve this community."

That deflated the activist, and we were able to have a frank meeting.

We took a barbershop owner from Cleveland with us to one of the meetings at the White House with the Department of American Innovation. White people don't realize how central the barbershops and the beauty parlors are to the black community. That's where the man on the street is able to engage with others in the black community, able to articulate, debate, and discuss a number of issues that are germane to the community. In that meeting, we talked about the problem of drugs, particularly the opioid fentanyl, in the black community, and President Trump's efforts to curtail its availability. Our barber friend, who'd had a preconceived opinion of this administration from listening to the left-wing media, went away with a totally different opinion of the White House and Donald Trump.

He said, "I can't believe it. This isn't what they tell us on CNN. This isn't what they're saying on MSNBC. They're making it out like these are a bunch of crackers up here that hate black people, and here they are asking us what they can do to better serve our people." He was pleasantly surprised.

He said, "Listen, when I go back, I'm going to have to let the people in the community know, 'It's not what you think it is.'"

He went back to his barbershop with its televisions. He left some of the TVs on CNN and put others on Fox—because, as he said, "I want to get a balance in this reporting."

I believe contributions like his are necessary, because he and others like him represent the man on the street. They can reach people that Trump could never reach.

The Bible says, "My people perish for lack of knowledge." Black people are told, "Don't listen to anything from the right; listen only to what the left has to say." The left is able to manipulate the masses through biased political propaganda—via CNN, MSNBC, and all the other left-leaning media organizations.

We had another meeting months later in the White House. We took some community leaders from Florida who had been Democrats for decades but had become frustrated with the Democratic Party.

They said, "We're willing to put party politics aside and work with this administration to help make black America great." We all sat down to discuss ways to improve the black community. They went away pleasantly surprised and thoroughly impressed by the level of cooperation from the White House. It also gave them a different opinion of this administration.

We had an Urban Revitalization Coalition meeting in Bridgeport, Connecticut. The room was full of Democrats, with the exception of Kareem and me. But our blackness still connected us. They asked us why we support Donald Trump, because conventional wisdom and logic say we shouldn't. It gave me the opportunity to make everyone aware of how I met Trump, and of the frank conversations that he and I have had over the years regarding matters of race. I told them that he has overperformed regarding the promises that he's made to the black community. There has been criminal justice reform that counteracts that Clinton crime bill, the one that disproportionately incarcerated African Americans. There has been prison reform in terms of sentencing reduction and equity. Hundreds of millions of dollars in grants have been dispersed to historically black colleges and universities (HBCUs). Opportunity zones have been created. We have the urban revitalization initiative. We have the lowest-ever unemployment statistics for the black community. It's easy for me to defend Trump now, because we can all look back and see what he has accomplished.

In that Bridgeport meeting, in a room full of Democratic political activists, one guy by the name of Ernie Newton—who had been a council member for decades—stood up and stood out. He said, "If we're all on the same ship, and there are some people on the top level and others on the bottom level, and the ship springs a leak, we're all going to go down." He added that it's imperative to accept the reality that Donald Trump is president, and urged people to work with this administration—because if this administration desires to work with us, why would we be dumb enough to refuse cooperation?

The ship analogy was a great one.

* * *

Trump has always expressed a genuine concern and a genuine interest in the African-American community.

Whenever something significant was passed, such as the opportunity zone legislation, the criminal justice reform legislation, the prison reform, or when the unemployment numbers were announced, he would always ask me if the black community was pleased.

He would say:

"We got the op zone bill passed."

"We've got the criminal justice reform passed."

"What does the African-American community think about it?"

"Are they pleased?"

He believed the African-American community had received the short end of the stick socially in America, primarily from the policies of the Democratic Party locally and nationally.

He would ask my opinion on a number of things regarding the African-American community, which I appreciate. He always included me in efforts and activities that involved the African-American community. He always made it a point to have me in the room at the signings and to acknowledge my contribution, which he didn't have to do, but I appreciate. When it came time for the signing of the First Step Act, I was there with him in the Oval Office. When it came time for the passage of the opportunity zones, I was there.

I was in the evangelical dinner meeting with him, and as he was speaking, he saw me out there and called me up, and had me standing next to him while he spoke. I was at a fundraiser event with him and he saw me out there, and he called me up on the stage and acknowledged me. We were at a Black History Month event, and he saw me out there. Out of all the hundreds of people who were in the room, he called me up on the stage and acknowledged my wife.

I see a lot of his efforts are geared toward unemployment, underemployment, and depressed living conditions, which he said to me were some of the main factors in the disenfranchisement of the black community back in 2011. He was very serious about what he said back then, that it wasn't just talk. He had not forgotten.

* * *

The black community is not as antagonistic toward the president as the media portrays it to be.

We just want the truth and a fair shake. We want an equal chance and equal treatment—equal opportunities and justice. Nothing more, nothing less, regardless of what the race hustlers try to say.

Once Trump became president, all the rioting and violence prevalent during the 2016 campaign stopped. That proves that there had been outside instigation and agitation. The fear mongering promoted in the black community has stopped, because we're able to look at some very real issues and see some very real results. We have not been put back into slavery. We have not all been locked up. We have not been oppressed by the Trump administration like the race hustlers on the left told us we would be. We have not been victimized by "whitelash." The Klan is not burning crosses on our lawns and lynching us.

I ran into a guy I know who owns a construction company.

He said, "Look, Pastor Scott. To be honest, when you first started saying this about Trump, I didn't believe you. I didn't like him. I didn't vote for him. But ever since he's become president, I've had more construction work than I've ever had. I'm staying a Democrat, but I'm voting for him."

That is what a lot of people in the black community are saying. Members of my congregation have said, "Pastor, ever since Trump has become president, my 401(k) plan is swelling." We see that his policies have helped the African-American community. As much as the left may try to deny it, it's the truth.

The narrative is beginning to shift.

The climate began to change after Trump became president and started accomplishing things. Early on in the primaries, my wife and I ran into political commentator Ana Navarro in the lobby of a New York City hotel. I recognized her, but she didn't know who I was.

I said, "What do you think about Trump?" She looked at me and, as I said, didn't know me. I could have been anybody. She just said, "Fuck Trump. Fuck Donald Trump." So much for objectivity. That just showed me the mindset that some have regarding Trump, and it made me feel a whole lot better about him winning the election. You know what's funny? All the hate that the left talks about goes from left to right. It doesn't go from right to left. None of the right-leaning pundits, contributors, or media personalities would say to me, "Fuck Hillary," or "I hate

Hillary." Or any other Democrat. They didn't say, "Fuck Bernie." The left-wing media stirred up racial tension, hate, antagonism, and animosity. It's sickening how members of the left-wing media would stand out in the street and look up in the air and scream and holler, protesting and wearing hats that were supposed to be vaginas. Madonna said she wanted to blow up the White House. Kathy Griffin posted a photo holding up a replica of Trump's decapitated head.

If someone on the right had talked about wanting to blow up the White House with Obama in it, or behead Obama or Hillary Clinton, there would have been a national outcry. Discrimination is bad, unless you're discriminating against a Trump supporter. You're not supposed to shame, bully, oppress, or antagonize anyone—unless it's a Trump supporter. The media tried to impress that mentality on America and has been very successful. The left-wing media has condoned mobs showing up at people's houses in the middle of the night and going to restaurants to stop those on the right from eating. You don't see people on the right doing that to people on the left.

I was walking with Kareem through the D.C. airport one time, and a guy came up and told me, "You ought to be ashamed of yourself." Before I could catch myself and remember that I am a pastor, a man of God, the street guy in me came out.

"What? Who're you talking to?"

Kareem and I began to walk up on the guy, but he hurried up and got into his Uber. As the car was pulling away, he said out the window: "History is not going to be kind to you."

I said, "Some people read history, some people write history, and some people make history. I'm one of the history makers; at least history will remember me."

But I didn't get a lot of pushback on the street in general. I was once at a gym where my grandson was playing basketball. A friend of mine said, "You know what's funny? I was talking to a group of guys, and they were talking about you. Talking badly about you. Then you walked in. I said, 'There he is right there. Do you want to say it to his face?' They all said no."

I said, "Where are they at?"

He pointed them out. I walked over to them and said, "How are you guys doing? Everybody alright?" They didn't say anything to my face.

The URC's efforts are going full steam ahead. As I write this, the initiatives for the black community that were in the planning stages are nearing execution. Everyone is motivated and optimistic. Everyone is encouraged about the direction that this country is proceeding in, despite all the opposition we're facing.

I recently had the privilege of flying on Air Force One for the first time. Belinda, Kareem, and I had been invited to accompany the president, who was going to speak at a historical black college to receive an award for his efforts with the First Step Act. At that event, the president said something that I believe should be our motto going forward. During his speech, he called me out and talked about how long my wife and I had been married. He listed some of his accomplishments. He spoke of criminal justice reform. He spoke of the Clinton crime bill. He spoke of prison reform. He spoke of sentencing reduction. He spoke of the HBCU activity, the opportunity zones, the lowest-ever unemployment, the urban revitalization.

Then he summed up by saying, "You know what, though? The best is yet to come."

The audience erupted in applause. It was the best-received line of the night. Afterward, I told the president, his speechwriter, those working on the 2020 campaign, and Jared, "I think we need to stay with that."

I'm optimistic about what the future holds for black America under the Trump administration. The Bible says, "The steps of a good man are ordered by the Lord."

When I think of great characters in the Bible, I think of Joseph and David in particular. I'm not comparing myself to them; I'm just using their stories as examples. God gave Joseph a dream of the throne while he was still young. He gave David a prophecy of the palace while he was still tending his father's sheep. God doesn't start at the beginning and work up to the end; God starts at the end and works back to the beginning. He started at Joseph's palace and worked back—through the prison, through the slavery, through the pit that he was thrown in, through the hate of his brothers. Every step that Joseph took was one that God had already taken before him. God knew what Joseph's end was going to be. While Joseph was in slavery and in prison, God saw him as the future pharaoh of Egypt.

David received the prophecy of becoming a king, and wound up running from Saul and hiding in caves. But even while he was in the cave, God said, "That's my king right there."

God already knew what he had in store for my wife and me when I was living a life of crime and she was a jazz singer. He said, "Those are my future pastors right there." When I was a young kid drinking and smoking and using drugs, when I was in the nightclubs, when I was in the military, when I met my wife, when I was doing whatever I was doing, God knew that I would wind up being an advisor to the president of the United States. Unlikely allies.

God already knew what he had in store for Donald Trump while he was building buildings, hosting television shows and beauty pageants, and living a celebrity lifestyle. God said, "That's my future president right there."

You cannot say Donald Trump's presidency is against God's will. The Bible says, "Anyone that is in authority is in authority by and through the will of God." God is going to have His way no matter what. He orchestrates and He choreographs. The Bible says, "Known unto God are all his works, from the beginning of the world."

The Bible says that God called a famine upon the entire land in order to cause the nation of Israel to wind up in Egypt. People who didn't seem to have anything to do with the nation of Israel were affected by this famine, in order for the purpose of God to prevail. I believe it was God's purpose for me to be at this critical juncture in our nation's history.

In the Bible, Esther's uncle tells her, "Who knows whether or not you were called to the kingdom for such a time as this." Esther wound up being the bride of a pagan king. God orchestrated her elevation into the position of that queenship. The first queen, Vashti, had to rebel against the king in order for him to displace her. Esther had to beat out many other competitors to obtain the queenship. She married outside her race, and I know people talked about her: "What is she doing? She's one of us. How could she side with them? How could she want to be his wife when he's one of the oppressors?" God was putting her in a unique position to be able to speak to power—to preserve the lives of her people and to be a benefit to her people.

Donald Trump is the most powerful man on the face of planet Earth. God has given me a unique position to be able to speak to power. I'm not going to despise that. Would I do it over again? Yes, I would. Would I do it differently? I can think of some things I would do differently. I wouldn't be as nice to some people.

I lost a lot of money, income, friends, members of my church. Subjected my wife and my family to criticism and controversy that they didn't ask for. Was the risk worth the reward? Absolutely. Were the antagonism, adversity, criticism, and ostracism worth it? Yes, they were.

I think that if I was able to influence the 8 percent of black Americans who voted for Trump in 2016, that if I was able to help tip the scales so that we could have criminal justice reform, prison reform, and sentencing reductions, it was worth it.

If I contributed to the lowest-ever unemployment numbers for the African-American communities, and I helped revitalization of black communities through the URC, it was worth it. If I played a small part in the creation of opportunity zones, it was worth it.

Would I do it over again? Yes, I would. In fact, I *want* to do it again. I think I'll do a better job in 2020 than I did in 2016. In 2016, I was just learning how to navigate. I had to learn the landscape on the fly. I know what not to do now; I know the terrain better. I have more knowledge and stronger relationships now. I think I'll be more effective in 2020 for this administration—which would by extension make me more effective for this country.

I think I'm a little more seasoned, a little wiser. I think I know my way around politics a little bit more. I'm by no means a politician, but I've always said that compared to church politics, these political politics came easy for me. I have a better grasp and a better understanding of both sides now, in the sense of government and community. I know what the man on the street is thinking, and I know what the man at 1600 Pennsylvania Avenue and the men up on the Hill are thinking. As a friend once said, I'm connected from the president of the United States to the junkie on the streets.

Not many people can make that boast.

I think that I can continue to build bridges, burning some along the way but building more. I'm able to be more discerning, because I can look at the media and have greater insight into what is real news and what is fake news.

I can understand the mindset of this administration. I can see how hard the people in this administration work. How much the Trump family has sacrificed for this. Trump didn't need this position, and I didn't need it either.

What do I think Donald Trump's motivation has been and still is? It's not the money; he had all of the money he needed before he started in politics. It wasn't the power. It wasn't the celebrity. It wasn't egomania.

When you're young, you look only toward your destiny: "What am I going to do when I become older? Am I going to be a success?" But as you get older, you start looking at your legacy: "What am I leaving behind? What have I left behind? What's going to happen to me when I die?"

I can offer only my opinion regarding Trump's motivation, for what it's worth.

Trump had all the success in the world, but a void still existed in his heart that needed to be filled. That void was public service. If you look back over decades, you can see that he has always been keen on politics and opinionated politically.

He wants to do right by Christianity, do right by the church world, and do right by the people of God, because he knows he's going to stand before God one day.

He wants to do right by the American people, because he loves this great country and he's proud to be an American. He wants to preserve, protect, and defend the Constitution of the United States to the best of his ability, and defend our country from enemies both foreign and domestic.

A lot of people would consider me to be a success in my field of endeavor. I am very happy and very satisfied, because I believe that there's no higher call than the call of God in a person's life. The call to the presidency is not higher than the call of God. The office of the president is not higher than the office of pastor, of any man of God.

I want my daughter, my grandchildren, and the great-grandchildren I'll never meet to know that their PawPaw participated in something historic, that their father or grandfather or great-grandfather was a friend and advisor to a billionaire who became president. That he did things to help this country and help its people.

The Trump 2020 campaign has launched a black coalition exclusively for Trump called Black Voices for Trump, in Atlanta, and has honored me with a seat on its board. It's encouraging to see others in and of the black community come forward to publicly declare their support for President Donald Trump. Seeing thousands come forward publicly to say, "We're standing with Donald Trump," is very encouraging. As I said at the launch of Black Voices for Trump, "Courage is contagious." The courage of a few brave blacks in 2016 has inspired the courage of thousands in 2020.

We need as many outspoken black public supporters and defenders of Trump as we can get. I have a healthy dose of self-esteem and self-respect. I've realized that you don't make your light shine any brighter by putting out somebody else's light.

I'm excited about Black Voices for Trump. I would love to think that in some small way, my contribution and the contributions of others who were pro-Trump when it wasn't popular to be pro-Trump led to its creation.

I'm optimistic that even more movements are going to emerge in the future that will elevate our community to a position of social and economic equality. African Americans throughout the nation will not be ashamed of their support for President Trump. His policies have bettered the black community, and no one can deny that.

I voted for him in 2016, and I'm going to vote for him in 2020. I supported him in the past, and I'm going to continue to support him in the present and future. I haven't been let down; in fact, he has exceeded my expectations.

One night at the Trump hotel, Corey Lewandowski was talking to my grandchildren. He said, "You guys are too young to realize it, but twenty-five, thirty, or thirty-five years from, you'll tell your kids and your grandkids what a great thing was accomplished, and that your grandfather helped make history."

Truth be told, it's been a helluva ride. And America needs to enjoy the ride that the Trump administration is taking it on. Trump's not only making America great again; he's making America fun again. The news media ought to thank him for ratings. The first thing Americans do every day is turn to the news, because we don't know what's going to happen. Every day in America is exciting. I get up and turn on the news because I don't want to miss a headline: "What did Trump say? What did Trump do?" He has made America fun again.

I want to ask those who are on the fence, who still harbor doubts about President Trump: What do you have to lose? You've got too much to gain. He's already given a taste of what he's capable of doing regarding our community, and it's only going to get better in the future.

The best is yet to come!